AF446103

# BLIND TRAVELER'S BLUES

A Douglas Abledan Novel

by

Robert P. Bennett

This story is fictional. The names and some of the locations of businesses have been changed.

All rights Reserved.
Copyright © 2011 by Robert P. Bennett
Cover Art © Karen L. Syed

Published by Enabling Words
Jericho, NY 11753
www.enablingwords.com

All rights reserved. No part of this book may be used or reproduced in any manner whatsoever without written permission, except in the case of brief quotations embodied in critical articles and reviews. The creation of this novel is due in no small measure to those who helped me accumulate the facts behind the fiction.

A story starts with a setting. I chose pre-Columbian Mexico. When I wanted to learn about the Chichimec people of that era, I asked Dylan J. Clark of Harvard University's Department of Anthropology. He read through early drafts of my preface, helping me create the image of a working dig site.

Good mysteries involve insidious methods of committing crimes. I chose poison. Turning to the internet to learn about obscure, deadly botanicals, I found excellent sources in the form of CJ Wilkes and Charlotte Leslie.

Shannon McNamara, from the National Corn Refiners Association, taught me about the ways we use corn and its by-products in every facet of society. With her guidance I developed the challenge I gave my characters.

Dr. Clayton Hollier, an agricultural pathologist from Louisiana State University, described for me the many deadly diseases that face our world's agricultural crops.

People like Gregg Fritsch, from NCR USA, find ways to balance the playing field for people with disabilities. When I needed to learn about devices that allow blind people to get through airports more easily, Gregg provided a wealth of information about voice recognition and motion detection.

No writer works in a vacuum. No story is perfectly written from inception. Grammar, spelling, word choice, and even scene arrangement is made better with the assistance of editors and beta readers. I had my share. My editors Mary

Linn Roby and Liz Borino granted me their vast expertise, patience, hard work, and advice.

Finally, to my mother, Audrey; my brothers, Jeff and Stephen; and my friends, Laura Cowan, Carol Casa, and Rob DiRe, my gratitude is undying for your love and patience while reviewing, and sometimes arguing about, sections of this story. You challenge me to be a better craftsman.

## *Two months ago*

Dr. Ramon Ramirez sat on the sun-baked ground hunched over a small piece of pottery. Using a painter's brush, he removed a layer of caked-on dirt and examined the fragment expectantly. With any luck, this site would hold a significant find, placing his name in the archeological history books.Several geologists theorized that in 2001 the earth's magnetic poles began to undergo a period of massive shifts, just as they did every few hundred thousand years. They said the tsunami off the coast of Sumatra in 2004 began as an earthquake caused by the shifting poles. Over time, the geologists claimed, the quakes would become more numerous and powerful, striking in places never before affected. It now seemed they were right.

Ramirez didn't care what caused the quakes. Neither geology nor seismology interested him. Though the increasing number and severity of quakes caused wide- scale destruction, in this case, by uncovering an ancient village, they proved beneficial. As a professor of archaeology at the University of Mexico for the past ten years, his name meant little outside the academic world. Now, if this expedition succeeded, he might have the chance to contribute something of major significance.

It took some time to convince the university to allow him to explore this site. The board members argued there were others with far more field experience. They examined his other expeditions, which did not bear much fruit. But, after a great deal of debate over his credentials, they granted him both funds and a small number of graduate students. He now competed against both time and research teams from other universities, all of them trying to find artifacts linking the site to a culture and giving it a place on the historical timeline.

Several hundred feet away, Luiz Garcia watched his mentor's activities like a radar dish fixed on its target. Mindful of spying eyes, he made his way to what appeared to be the remnants of an ancient wall poking out of the dirt. There wasn't much left, but the construction seemed similar to the wall surrounding the city of Tenayuca, the capital of the Chichimec Empire. Finally, he'd found something to be excited about.

Dusting off a small section inscribed with a series of petroglyphs, he began to copy the symbols into a leather-bound journal, planning to compare them later to several texts the group brought along on the trip. Two images in particular interested him. One depicted a red-tinged man. Though faded by time, the figure seemed to be wearing a headdress in the shape of a bird. The other appeared to be a stylized hummingbird and might be a representation of Huitzilopochtli, the patron-god of the Chichimec. These two images could prove to be very important. They could help to establish the placement of this group of native Mexicans in a region farther north than previously suspected.

Garcia took off his silver-framed glasses, rubbed the lenses with his shirt, and replaced them on the bridge of his nose. Surveying the surrounding area, he tried to envision the settlement the way it might have appeared hundreds of years earlier, with men, women, and children living a simple, organic lifestyle, going about their daily business.

Garcia wasn't a fan of the 21st century. There were too many "conveniences" for his taste. He felt more comfortable in the past. Pursuing a career wherein he could explore ancient civilizations provided a counterbalance to his discomfort. Of course, his work was a contradiction of sorts. Archeologists the world over relied more and more on science and technology to do their job. Discoveries of sites like this one, through a natural occurrence like an earthquake, rarely occurred.

Sixteen archaeology students were working this site, together with him and Ramirez. Garcia could see Joan Aquilla peering through a theodolite in the southwest corner. She seemed to be having difficulty keeping the three legs of the device solidly planted on the uneven ground. Farther north, Roberto Estaban shook a screen over a tarp lying on the ground, pausing periodically to examine clumps of earth more closely. Trying not to disturb the dirt, or the strings used to separate the site into quadrants, Garcia made his way to where Aquilla labored.

"There doesn't appear to be much here, does there?"

Brushing a lock of long, black hair back from her face, and shielding her eyes from the sun's blazing rays, she stared up at him.

"Be patient, Luiz. We haven't been here very long. This is a big site. There's a lot of ground to cover."

"I can't help it," he told her. "Waiting around until Ramirez uncovers something big enough to suit his ego isn't what I consider true scientific research."

The woman sighed. "Don't think of it as something for Ramirez. Think of it as an expansion of your own knowledge of the people who lived here. How did you manage on your other digs?"

"I don't know. It's hot, and the wind is kicking dirt in my eyes. The other digs weren't like this. The sites were more compact, and the work went quicker."

"Well, that was then and this is now, and you're going

to have to adjust to this environment and this job. You can do it; I have faith. Now you better get back to work before Dr. Ramirez catches you loafing. You know how he is."

Garcia knew only too well. Today's find could be payback time.

* * *

When night finally arrived, Garcia flopped onto his cot, exhausted from the day's heat and activity. Being an archaeobotanist wasn't shaping up to be anything like he'd imagined. Where were the dark secrets? The intrigue? As a child he watched the Indiana Jones movies until the discs wore out. Now, decades later, he longed to follow in Jones's footsteps. He craved the adventure of discovering ancient civilizations, even when they were fraught with occasional danger. But, so far most of the dig sites he worked on were boring. Though the occasional interesting artifact, like the one he unearthed today, did reveal itself, for the most part he languished. The amount of work involved in finding so little was more than he'd bargained for. He closed his eyes and tried to sleep, only to hear someone slip into his tent.

*What is it now?*

Garcia rolled over and turned on his lantern, blinking several times to force his eyes to adjust to the light.

"Are you awake, Luiz?"

Garcia loved Aquilla's spontaneity, but tonight wasn't a good night for it. Not on the day he'd made one of the most important discoveries of his career; and certainly not when he'd decided to keep the discovery from Ramirez.

"Are you crazy, Joan? It's late. What if someone saw you?"

Tying the tent flap behind her, she walked toward him, slowly unbuttoning her shirt, and sat down on the edge of his cot.

"Shh. I'm worried about you. It's clear to everyone you aren't happy. Even Ramirez notices and you know he doesn't pay much attention when he's involved with a project."

Garcia pulled in a gulp of air and let it out slowly. "I'm fine, just a bit on edge."

"But why? You had a good day today. Those petroglyphs you found are very interesting. They could help prove Ramirez's theory."

Garcia's lips tightened at the mention of the man's name.

"I don't like that guy, and I don't want my discoveries, whatever they are, linked to him."

"I know he can be a bit self-important, but he's a good teacher too. I think if you're patient, as I've suggested before, you'll learn a lot from him. You're a good researcher

in your own right. You'll find something to distinguish yourself, either here or someplace else. I'm sure of it. Now, do we have to spend the night talking about Ramirez?"

Garcia felt the tension in his muscles fade. Somehow, like magic, this woman had the ability to help him keep things in perspective. He leaned forward to kiss her neck.

"Okay, no more talk about Ramirez or archeology. I have something interesting to show you, but it can wait until the morning."

"I think you have something to show me right now." She reached behind his head to turn off the lantern, and kissed him deeply, her long hair encircling his face.

***

In the morning, a strong wind beat on the canvas, and heavy footfalls beat down the ground just outside.

"Get under the blanket and don't move," Garcia whispered.

When he'd accepted their application, Ramirez made it clear to the two of them any on-site fraternization would not be tolerated. This trip, he'd said, would be about the work, not some romantic getaway. But, Garcia saw the statement as just one more example of the man's heavy- handedness.

"Don't worry," Aquilla said. "I tied the tent closed last night, remember? Hurry up and put your pants on."

Throwing off the blanket, Garcia paused long enough to kiss her again before reaching for his clothes. The wind rose now, billowing out one side of the tent.

"When I get rid of whoever it is I have something to show you."

"Again? What kind of woman do you think I am, Señor?"

Giggling, she pushed him through the tent opening.

"Garcia," Ramirez bellowed. "Why aren't you out here working?"

"I'm sorry. Doctor, I was just finishing my journal entry. I wanted to make sure I had everything down from yesterday before I forgot any details."

Ramirez looked at the younger man through slitted eyelids. "You should have done so last night, before retiring. Never mind now. Just hurry up and get out to the site. There are still plenty of discoveries to be made. History won't wait forever, you know."

"Yes, Sir."

Garcia waited until Ramirez disappeared halfway down

the hill before darting back into the tent. Pulling down the blanket, he paused for a long moment, savoring the beauty of his lover's bronzed, naked body, before telling her to hurry and get dressed.

"I don't want anyone coming in here and seeing you naked," he said. "And don't scream when I show you what I found yesterday."

Turning his back to her, he undid the lock on his duffle bag.

"You can't tell anyone about this. I'm serious. No one. Promise me. Everyone thinks I found only those petroglyphs yesterday, but I found something more important."

Reaching into the bag, he pulled out a cloth-wrapped object, cradling it in the crook of his arm before passing it to her, saying, "Take it. Look at it."

Aquilla gingerly unfolded the burlap. Inside laid a pear-shaped terracotta jar, about twelve inches tall. Deeply cut lines created an intricate pattern along the surface.

"Luiz, it's beautiful," she cried. "You can even see remnants of some of the pigments they used. See here? This pattern may have been a depiction of Xilonen. And this one could be Mixcoatl."

Garcia smiled proudly. Finally, someone gave him the credit he deserved.

"Where did you find this? You have to show it to Ramirez. It's just the kind of artifact he's been looking for."

"I'm not showing it to anyone except you. It's mine, my claim to archeological history. I found it buried next to the wall of petroglyphs. Those are Chichimec characters carved into it. I checked in the books. That means they did inhabit the region, just as Ramirez has postulated. And this," he went on, pointing to one particular glyph, "suggests inside the jar there might be remnants of some kind of grain."

"But, Luiz, that's exactly why you have to show it to him. He'll be thrilled, and I'm sure he'll give you credit for finding it."

"You think so?" He raised his voice so she could hear him over the howling wind. "With his ego? My name will never come up."

"Now who's being egotistic?"

"Let Ramirez have all the ruins and other artifacts he wants. This is *my* find. I'm an archaeobotanist. If there is any grain inside the jar, it would suggest the Chichimec practiced some form of agriculture, that they were more than just the warriors and hunters most archeologists and anthropologists believe they were. Now, give it back to me so I can hide it again."

Aquilla shook her head. "I can't, Luiz. It's not right."
Garcia reached for the jar just as a thunderous gust threatened to tear the tent from its moorings. His fingers missed their target. The vessel smashed to the ground. A cloud of something akin to dust momentarily hovered in the air before pelting their faces and whisking out of tent. Although he did not know it, his world now teetered on the brink of change, and not for the better.

Blind Traveler's Blues

# PART ONE
## Vacation

# CHAPTER ONE
*Day 1*

An earthquake jolted Douglas awake. He rolled onto his back and waited for it to settle down, relieved to have been shaken out of a recurring nightmare in which he watched himself being shot and blinded. This one felt fairly weak. Even still, being outside would potentially have been dangerous. Inside he felt safe, at least from falling debris. Then, too, the increasing regularity of these earthquakes provided an unexpected benefit. They didn't need "setting" like an alarm clock did. But, he still lost sleep.

Rather than try to get more sleep, and risk the nightmare's return, Douglas decided to get up. Today promised to be a busy day. Tomorrow he'd leave on his vacation and he still had a lot to do. Climbing out from under the covers, he reached for his robe, which lay purposefully tangled up and thrown on the floor the night before. In the morning it was a challenge to see how long it took to unscramble the cloth, as if being blind didn't present challenges enough.

The robe secured around him, he walked into the kitchen where a pouch of coffee and two slices of bread sat in their respective machines. Pouring water into the coffee maker, he turned it on, and pushed down the toaster's handle. While he waited for the pings signaling the completion of both tasks, he dressed and turned on his computer to check e-mail and listen to the headlines from *The New York Times* website.

"Today is September sixteen, two thousand and twenty-one," a feminine voice announced once the machine booted.

The weather today would, it appeared, be sunny and cool, a refreshing relief from the summer's heat. Iran and Iraq were still in negotiations to remove the border between them and become one large country. New Orleans laid in ruins from yet another hurricane. This time five thousand people died.

Most of the headlines had become fairly standard, but one caught Douglas's attention. He told the machine to read the text of an article reporting on progress archeologists were making at a dig site on the Mexico side of the Texas/Mexico border. An earthquake in the region several months earlier uncovered what appeared to be Indian ruins. Douglas had always been interested in ancient civilizations and architecture. This article, part of a series he'd been following, didn't disclose much information on the developing story. Nevertheless, he told the computer to mark it, then gulped down the coffee, wolfed down the toast, and clipped his BTI Systems' IS3 Navigator to his belt before rushing out the door.

* * *

"Hey Doug."

*Shoot!*

Being cornered by Sid Coltrane was something Douglas always hoped to avoid. It was an unrequited fantasy. Not a day went by when his boss didn't corner him somewhere in the office. To make matters worse, the name Coltrane called him by, "Doug," grated on his nerves. He'd hated it ever since childhood.

"Come on over to my office for a second, will you please? I want to ask you something."

Douglas hated being summoned to his boss's office. A toxic cloudbank hung in there. Coltrane, a chain smoker, refused to give his addiction a rest despite the legal codes he broke by smoking in a public building. Unrepentant, he once explained if he must be confined to an office for an entire day no one would stop him from smoking in it, especially since the recurring earthquakes made a future life uncertain for anyone.

"Come in and close the door, please," Coltrane said in the squeaky voice many people found irritating, but which Douglas thought fit the man precisely. "Listen, I know today is your last day before vacation. You're going to Chicago, right?"

"I thought about going to New Orleans," Douglas told him. "They have a better reputation for Blues, but this is hurricane season and they've experienced quite a few bad ones in recent years. I'd prefer to steer clear of those."

"Since you're going there anyway, how about doing some company business? You're the best software guy we have and there's a guy who could really use your expertise. I don't think he's too swift, if you know what I mean."

"This is supposed to be my vacation, Sid. I haven't had one of those in a long time, you know. I don't want to think about computers, or New York, while I'm gone."

Coltrane exhaled slowly. "So you won't do me and the company you've worked for for years, the company that kept you on and gave you a new job after your 'accident,' a little favor? I thought you'd be a bit more loyal. I thought you wouldn't mind helping your friend Sid out of a jam. It's not like you'd be going out of your way."

"Please don't pull the friendship card on me, Sid. It's not fair. We're friends, but this is my vacation. You know there's been a lot going on the past few weeks."

"I know, Doug, and I wouldn't normally ask you to do this during your time off. But if you don't, I'll have to send someone else there this week. And, as you may know, Datascan Corporation isn't faring so well right now. We really can't afford to pay someone to go."

"You know, if I were a suspicious person, I might think you planned this and timed it to coincide with my trip to Chicago. But, I'll do it, as long as I'm going to be there anyway."

"Thank you, Doug. I won't forget this and neither will the company. I'll even see if we can front you a bit of a bonus, so you have some extra cash while you're there. I can't promise, but I'll see what I can do."

Douglas fled his boss's office before the man took the opportunity to ask for anything else.

*That's just great! At least I'll get something out of it.*

* * *

Orlando Hernandez rubbed the sleep from his eyes, and ran his fingers through his thick, dark hair before slowly following the other passengers out of the bus. Swallowing hard, he tried to ignore the knot of fear tightening in his stomach. He had never been this far from his family or his farm, but he felt a pressing need to be here in Mexico City. He needed answers. After listening to reports on the radio, he knew travelling to the city held the only chance of getting them.

Hernandez scanned the square. He had never seen so many people in such a small space. Some, like him, were relatively well-dressed while others wore little more than rags. He tried to listen to several of the conversations around him, but there were so many people the chatter became unintelligible. Intense emotion, however, hung in the air like a storm cloud about to burst. Mostly people were just plain angry, but a good bit of sadness hung in the air too. No one escaped unscathed from the effects of the corn disease.

On the other side of the square stood a tall, red-bricked building with a white balcony from which, he imagined, the President would probably speak. Hernandez wanted to get as close as possible without getting crushed by the crowd. A difficult task, but perhaps possible, with some luck. Finally, he saw a spot and spent the next ten minutes pushing through the sea of flesh to get there.

Soon after reaching his vantage point, silence washed over the crowd and President Hasta appeared.

"My fellow Mexicans, we are in a period of crisis," he began, leaning heavily on his lectern. "Our corn crop is being wiped out by disease. Our neighbors to the north have not been able to provide us with enough to make up for the losses we've suffered. Each of you," he pointed into the crowd, "has been called upon to make great sacrifices. It is not easy for me, your President, to ask that of you. Because of the shortage, prices on all corn-related products have risen. As a result, I have instituted a cap on the price of corn and corn products. Furthermore, your government is working to stem the tide of greed..."

"Your price caps mean nothing if my family starves to death," someone in the crowd shouted.

The crowd roared its agreement.

"It saddens me to say this, but yes, there have been many deaths due to starvation in recent days."

"We cannot afford your prices," another man bellowed.

Hasta cleared his throat.

"I know the price is high, but it is the best we can do under present conditions."

"It is too high," someone cried. "We need help, not speeches or apologies."

"And you will get help as soon as it can be arranged. I promise."

"We've heard these promises before. The price keeps going up."

"The price of corn and cornmeal will not continue to rise. I've seen to that." He spread his arms toward the crowd. "My fellow Mexicans, I need to ask for your patience and cooperation during this crisis."

"We are out of patience."

Suddenly a large ball of packed mud arced through the air and landed with a soft splat at Hasta's feet. Instantly three men in black suits shot into the crowd, grabbed a short, round man dressed in off-white linen and pulled him out of the square.

"There is no reason for this kind of activity," Hasta declared. "Are we not civilized people? Can't we discuss our problems without resorting to such outbursts? I understand your frustration. But please remember, as your president, I am only here to help make your lives easier."

He no sooner finished speaking when a bloated corn cob struck his forehead, knocking him off balance.

"Easier? This is what we're left to eat."
The assembled mass of flesh erupted into a conflagration of rage. Two men dressed in black quickly pulled the stunned man back into the building.

## CHAPTER TWO
*Day 2*

The cab stopped with a screech, yanking Douglas out of his daydream.

"Hey, buddy, we're here. Kennedy Airport. Delta terminal. Come on, I can't sit here all day. You getting out or what?"

Doors opened. Closed. Douglas felt a cool breeze and smelled ethanol and oil as the driver helped him out of the cab and handed him his luggage, two heavy bags.

"What do I owe you?"

"That'll be fifty bucks even. I just need your thumb print, and a verbal authorization for the tip."

The fee seemed high considering the distance, but other companies quoted him more. He put down the bags and thrust his right hand in the direction of the driver's voice. He'd thought about paying in cash but, even with the new currency imprinted with textured ink so blind people could distinguish between denominations; he often found it easier to use his thumb.

"Tip?"

"Of course. Five dollars."

The driver grumbled something under his breath. Rather than engaging in what would no doubt end up being an argument, Douglas ignored the undoubtedly rude comment.

"Five bucks, huh? Okay. Fine. Just give me your thumb and let me get out of here."

The man didn't wait for Douglas to respond. Instead, he abruptly grabbed Douglas's hand, then mashed his thumb onto a small, greasy surface.

After retrieving his abused finger, Douglas doffed his hat at the driver, picked up his bags again, and turned away from the cab. In retrospect, he decided, requesting a cab with a driver, even such a rude one, instead of one of the new driverless models seemed to be a good idea. Retrieving his luggage from a driverless cab probably would have proved difficult.

"Do you need help with those? I'll check you in. What's your name? Where are you going?"

"Douglas Abledan. I'm traveling with Delta Airlines, flight sixteen forty-four to Chicago."

"I'll need to see some I.D"

Douglas pulled out his wallet and opened it.

"Here's my Non-Driver Identification Card. You'll have to forgive me, but I can't tell if it's a good likeness or not."

He thought about telling the man the picture had been taken after his accident, but decided the information would have raised questions he didn't feel like dealing with right now.

"You need help getting your boarding pass or anything?"

"Well, when I called ahead and said I was blind, I was told someone from the airline would help me."

"That's probably true, but they won't know you're here until you reach the ticket counter. The airlines don't have people waiting at the front door of the terminals. If you ask me, it's kind of rude, but they don't consider that people with disabilities sometimes travel alone."

*No, of course not. That would be the intelligent thing to do.*

"In that case, yes. I would appreciate assistance."

"Coming right up. Sir, while you're waiting, would you please step out of the way? We're a bit busy here today. I don't want you to get trampled by all these crazy people."

Douglas reached behind him, searching for the wall of the building. He took a few steps until his hand touched concrete, and then a few more until his back rested against it. Reaching into his pocket, his fingertips hunted for the smooth, cylindrical object he knew always rested there waiting to be called into service. Finally encircling it, he pressed the activator switch. The device warmed up quickly and, in a moment, he felt the familiar vibration indicating the sonic cane stood ready to perform its task.

He hated using the cane. Pushing the switch initiated an inescapable mind game he always felt destined to lose. Whenever he turned the cane on he catapulted back into the rehabilitation facility, helpless and in need.

Members of the staff at the Hecksher Rehabilitation Campus, in Hartford, Connecticut, were all very kind, and their goal of empowering newly blinded patients certainly seemed like a worthy one, but all he thought about in those early days of darkness was how weak his new disability made him. He lived all his life, over forty years, without needing any kind of assistance. Now, he often felt trapped, and in need.

Douglas lived at the Campus for five months. After being pronounced physically stable, he'd been released from the hospital. But, his doctor insisted, because his body had undergone a major change, he needed to learn how to live in a new way. Finally he acquiesced, if only to shut the man up, and was transferred to the Campus. Through many hours of therapy sessions, geared toward helping him adjust to being blind, he learned useful skills such as how to read Braille, count money by the way the bills were folded, dress himself, and use technology to make his life easier.

Some of the lessons, like how to use a cane to move around his environment, were simply annoying. He hated the ungainly, inelegant piece of wood and often threw it in frustration. Using it produced loud noises, invariably hurting his ears. He recognized the need for this kind of assistance. However, a few months later, when presented with the possibility of using a sonic cane, he jumped at the opportunity.

While retaining many of the same flaws inherent in a standard, white cane, this device wasn't quite so noisy. More importantly, it emitted an invisible beam, so its user looked less needy, less blind. Unfortunately, the device proved to be of limited use. Unlike the navigator, which he'd bought nine months after leaving the Campus, the sonic cane could neither tell him street names, nor distinguish between objects and people. It couldn't even accurately measure how far away an object stood.

But, because they depended on unobstructed communication with the global positioning satellites orbiting the Earth, the navigators were both virtually useless indoors and at getting around small objects. A key component, the device's mapping software, both fixed a user's position and told him of potential obstacles lying in his path. The signals transmitted between the satellites and the device he wore on his belt, where they turned objects into audible beeps, something called textured sound. No two objects, be it a tree or a building, produced the same sound.

After about ten minutes, Douglas felt a tug on his shirt sleeve, pulling him from his thoughts.

"You're the blind guy waiting for an escort?" someone demanded in a harsh, rapid voice. "I'm Irving. First things first. Let's get you to the ticket kiosk inside the terminal."

Automatic doors whooshed closed behind him as, with Irving's help, Douglas walked into the building.

"Here we are," Irving said. "Touch the machine and it will recognize you and pull up your travel information. It's pretty cool."

Douglas reached forward until his fingers met a hard surface. After a moment he felt a vibration. Apparently his fingerprints were being scanned.

*This is more convenient than speaking with a human.*

"Here's the earphone," Irving said, pressing a small, plastic item into Douglas's free hand. "You'll need it so you can communicate privately with the kiosk."

"Hello, Douglas Abledan," a mechanized voice said once he had fitted the earphone in his ear. "I'm Delta Airlines Ticketing Kiosk six-thirty-two. I have your information, but for security purposes, I need you to confirm it for me. What is your reservation number?"

"782sjk," Douglas said into the headset.

"That's correct. One moment and I will deduct the funds for the ticket from your bank account."

Douglas waited patiently while the machine performed the transaction. When it finished, he heard a sharp beep.

"Thank you, Mr. Abledan. You are on Delta Airlines flight number sixteen forty-four, New York to Chicago, which leaves from gate number forty-eight in one hour and ten minutes. Do you need directions to the gate?"

"I have a guide."

"I'm sorry, but I don't understand. Please speak slowly and clearly. Do you need directions to the gate?"

*Someone should upgrade your software.* "Yes," he replied, a bit louder than he'd intended.

"Very well. To get to gate forty-eight go down the hall, take the elevator to the second floor, turn left, and walk two hundred feet. The gate is on the right side of the hallway. Your boarding pass is being printed now. Please take it from the slot below and to your left. Thank you for flying Delta Airlines."

"Shall we go?"

Douglas jumped at the sound of the man's voice behind him. He had gotten used to hearing the voice of the machine.

"We're going to gate forty-eight. Your machine is great. Have you had it here long?"

"Hmm, I'd say we've had the kiosks for about two years now. They're very popular, especially with people in your, umm, situation. We had earlier models, but they didn't work as well. The interface wasn't well thought out. Interacting with it wasn't a smooth process."

"I guess a lot has changed since I took a plane last," Douglas admitted. "You know, Irving, it really is better if I hold onto you rather than you holding onto me. I'd feel more comfortable."

Walking through the terminal proved to be an unpleasant challenge. Even with a guide running interference, Douglas found himself constantly bumped into. Most of the people didn't bother to apologize before rushing off. While making plans to take this trip he considered, with dread, the possibility of having this exact experience. Even walking through the city during rush hour felt better. There, at least, his navigator made it easier to avoid people. And, the terminal seemed bigger than when he had his sight, although whether because of his guide's slow pace or because he couldn't see the path they walked along he couldn't be sure. Either way, getting to the gate seemed like an endless journey.

* * *

Dr. Cara Cordelia sat behind her desk in Cornell University's agricultural department, her head resting on her folded arms. Last night's work in the lab proved to be long and fruitless, just as it had virtually every night since discovery of the site in Mexico three months ago. Since then, the disease spread like wildfire, killing one third of the country's corn crop.

*Why couldn't they be more careful?*

She was not an archaeologist, but even she knew you needed to take precautions with any new discovery. Rushing into it, letting emotion outweigh scientific judgment, courted disaster.

Truth be told, there had been no way to know this would happen, no way to know a disease buried for so long would not only awaken but also begin to spread. But, what to do about it no one knew. So far, cursory examination of plant samples provided few answers. The disease exhibited the droopy, black-spotted leaves prominent in several modern-day rust infections, but it also produced the bloated and grayish galls common in many smut diseases. No present-day organism exhibited both symptoms.

Finally, about a month ago, an eager and resourceful student located a book holding a diagram of an ancient maize plant, depicting the same symptoms, together with a single sentence describing the disease as incurable at the time it existed. There were also historical records of a plant-eating disease causing a famine which possibly contributed to the demise of the Chichimec Indians of Mexico. Attributing the outbreak of the new infection to an archaeological site attributed to the group made sense.

Mexican officials asked for help from the US Department of Agriculture, and the word spread from there. Each of the major universities with recognized expertise in plant pathology took up the challenge of finding a cure, but so far the researchers remained clueless. A meeting, to be held at the University of Illinois' Chicago facilities, had been called for leaders in the field and Cordelia agreed to attend. But that first meeting led to another, and another, leaving her little time to devote to her own work until now, exhausted both physically and mentally, she found herself no closer to finding answers.

She raised her head when a knock sounded on the door and a thin, young man with long brown hair, haphazardly combed, appeared.

"Excuse me, Doctor," he said, handing her a large, blue, ceramic mug. "Here's the peppermint tea you asked for. You know, you really should think about calling it a day. You don't want to miss your flight. Chicago is waiting for you."

Thanking him, Cordelia looked at her new watch, pushed a button, and watched the display change from the time of day to two digits indicating her blood sugar level. Ninety. That accounted for her light-headedness. It was a relief not to have to prick her skin. A Type I diabetic, she'd suffered through the prick of sharp needles several times a day since childhood. Taking a sip of the tea, she momentarily relished in its warmth.

"I suppose you're right," she said, yawning. "I'm not getting anything done here anyway. Maybe I can get some work done on the plane. Change of scenery and all that, you know."

"Some sleep might help you think things through, Doctor. You've been pulling crazy hours, even worse than a grad student like me. Besides, if you're lucky you'll sleep great on the plane. There's something about having no distractions at thirty-five thousand feet that is incredibly relaxing."

"I hate flying and never can relax when I'm so far above solid ground. I find work keeps my mind off the fact I'm inside a winged bomb liable to go off at any time."

"Forgive me for saying this, Doctor, but you sound like my grandmother." He grinned. "There's nothing safer than flying. The odds of the plane exploding are like a gazillion to one."

"Is that so? Then why don't real people fly them anymore? There's got to be some reason they stopped using real pilots and replaced them with computers."

"You mean nav-computers? It's simple economics. Even before the recession of 2009 the airlines realized using real people was expensive."

"We have the same discussion each time I have to fly somewhere," Cordelia reminded him. "You have your opinion, I have mine. I guess telling you I am older and wiser doesn't change your mind."

"Nope. But I like to hear you say it. Now you better go save the world."

Dorn grinned as he left the room, but there was something in his eyes, a glint Cordelia didn't like. Was he mocking her? No. She must be wrong. Still, she couldn't shake the feeling something was amiss.

* * *

Joshua Dorn walked across the Ag Quad reflecting, not for the first time, on how he'd miss seeing the end result of the plans he and others began formulating months earlier. Still, it was enough to know he did his small part. As he walked down Tower Road a sly grin came to his lips. Turning onto Judd Falls Road, the grin became a broad smile. By the time he arrived at Plantations Road, he'd started whistling.

Once back in his apartment, he picked up the phone and pressed the top speed dial button. It would take about an hour for Cordelia to travel from Ithaca to New York City, and her flight didn't depart for ninety minutes. Barring delays, two and a half hours remained to make sure everything would be ready when she arrived. The right flight attendant must walk the aisle on the plane to Chicago. If she weren't, the plan would hit a snag. There was too much to lose.

The phone rang five times before a young woman answered.

"This is Joshua," he said. "Are you ready? You got yourself assigned to the flight, didn't you?"

"Calm down, Josh," the woman said, in the slightest of Americanized Japanese accents. "You're going to have a stroke if you keep worrying so much."

"Well? Are you ready for the flight?"

"What flight?" She giggled. "Today is my day off. I slept in this morning, then got my nails done. They're the prettiest color pink. You should see them. In an hour I'm going to get my hair cut."

"Liz, are you on the flight or not?" The woman could be exasperating when she wanted to be, but he still loved her.

"Stop worrying, silly. Of course I'm on the flight."

Slamming down the phone, Dorn began pacing the apartment. A lot depended on what happened next.

* * *

Douglas sat on the Boeing super jet, listening to the rhythmic sound of the turbines spinning. His feet tickled from the vibration of the floor. With the flight delayed by an hour he couldn't do anything but sit and wait, passing the time listening to snippets of conversation, mostly complaints with which he empathized. He had been looking forward to this vacation, but so far he felt disenchanted.

Running his fingers through his hair, he realized an appointment with his barber was overdue. It'd been over two months since the last one but, with Sid breathing down his neck at the office, Eddie, his friend and favorite hotdog vendor, still recuperating from being shot, and the police constantly calling with more questions about his "accidental" involvement in the Haggerty murder, life kept him too busy to make the call. The episode thankfully, finally over, he'd been trying to forget it, but getting back on track seemed an elusive endeavor.

*Well, it's not worth worrying about now.*

"Excuse me," a woman said. "Can I squeeze in? I'm in the window seat."

"I'm sorry," he said, stepping into the aisle to let her pass. "I'm a bit lost in my own thoughts, I guess. And, of course, I didn't see you standing there."

"What do you mean, 'of course, I didn't see you?'"

"I'm blind, but I should have known you were standing there. Your perfume is lovely."

After the woman settled into her seat, Douglas felt her reach for, and tighten, her seatbelt.

"So, I guess we're both off to Chicago. Are you as nervous about the trip as I am?"

"Nervous? No, what makes you think that?"

"You pulled your seatbelt extra tight. You don't know anything about this flight the rest of us don't, do you?"

"Well, no, I'm fine. I don't like flying, that's all. And, I really don't want to go on this trip. I'm only going to Chicago to attend a meeting I was talked into attending."

"I understand. In some ways I'm looking forward to it, and not in others. I haven't been on a plane or out of New York, for that matter, in over two years. It'll kind of be a new experience for me. Suffice it to say this will be my first trip since losing my sight. But, I've been rude. Allow me to introduce myself. My name is Douglas Abledan."

"I'm Cara Cordelia. Do you mind me asking if an accident or disease caused your blindness? I'm a doctor, of sorts."

"People only learn by asking questions, Dr. Cordelia. I was the victim of a shooting. I was struck in the head by a bullet which wasn't intended for me. It was a drive-by. Wrong place. Wrong time. That sort of thing. The police never caught the shooter. And, as far as I could tell, never really tried very hard."

Douglas knew his tone barely hid his anger. When the woman didn't respond, he realized she must be searching for something comforting to say. After an uncomfortably long moment, she cleared her throat.

"Please, forgive me, Mr. Abledan, but I really don't want to be conscious when we take off," she told him. "Can we talk later?"

The sound of the plane's engines grew louder. Now it wasn't just the floor vibrating. Douglas's seat rocked, too. After a moment the plane began to taxi down the runway. A gentle hiss from the air-conditioning jets acted like white noise, blocking out the voices of the other passengers. Douglas sat silently, alone with his thoughts.

*I must be crazy, taking a trip all alone, to a place I've never been. What if I can't get around? What if the navigator maps aren't accurate? Or, what if there's another glitch in the system?*

Douglas's fingers wandered to his navigator. He caressed the smooth, seamless surface, recalling when he'd first learned of the device's existence.

"It's been exhaustively tested, Douglas," the counselor

from the Campus had said during his follow-up visit. "It will make your life much easier." The current generation of navigators, she said, was flawless. But, she was wrong. The Haggarty incident proved it. Ironically, because of a glitch in the system he had witnessed the murder and, ultimately, solved the case.

* * *

Liz Ito stood inside the plane's cramped lavatory trying to straighten her uniform. The one she had intended to wear still hung at the dry cleaners, the victim of a foul-up with the claim ticket. The one she had on now didn't fit quite right anymore. It covered her in all the right places, but without much cloth to spare.

*That's all I need, a uniform that invites gawking by aerial perverts.*

Taking a small vial from her coat pocket, she unscrewed the cap and sniffed the sweet, minty aroma of its contents. Scrunching her nose, she replaced the cap, hesitating briefly before returning the vial to her pocket. This had to be done, Dorn insisted, but he hadn't said she had to like doing it.

* * *

Douglas felt the seat next to him move abruptly. Cordelia coughed a few times, as if trying to restart her lungs. True to her word, if her breathing demonstrated anything, she had been sleeping deeply for the past half hour.

"Sleep well?"

"How long was I out? Where are we?"

Douglas felt for his watch and pushed the voice-activator button.

"The time is 4:07 p.m.," a tinny voice announced.

"We're about halfway there," Douglas added.

"That's all? Damn! I wanted to sleep most of the trip. What am I going to do now?"

"Well, I could play my harmonica for you," Douglas suggested with an impish grin.

Suddenly, the plane rocked back and forth. Douglas grabbed his seat to stay balanced.

"Great," Cordelia said, "all I need is turbulence!"

"No big deal, Doctor. It's been awhile, but I doubt I've ever been on a flight that wasn't a bit rocky. We'll be fine. The airways between New York and Chicago aren't nearly as bumpy as others I've been on."

"I'm glad you think so, Mr. Abledan," she yelped. "So, what brings you on this bumpy ride to Chicago?"

"Strictly pleasure. I want to see the city and listen to some good Blues. At least that was the plan before my boss gave me an assignment."

"See the city? No offense, but you're blind. I can understand listening to music, but seeing the sights?"

"It's more a matter of feeling, hearing, and smelling. Since my accident, I've come to rely more on my remaining senses. For example, ever since I was young I've had a strong sense of smell, but now my nose helps me navigate the world around me. I can even, sometimes, tell how close I am to a restaurant or a body of water simply by the aroma."

Douglas stopped abruptly when he heard a deep, muffled rumbling coming down the aisle toward them.

"We're about to have a visitor, I think."

"A visitor?"

Douglas held up his hand as a minty aroma floated into his nose.

"Excuse me. Would you like a beverage?"

"A strong cup of peppermint tea is just what I need to take the edge off," Cordelia replied, passing over a small packet. "Would you pour the water over this teabag for me, please?"

After a few moments, Douglas heard the flight attendant pouring the water. The aroma, as the cup passed by him, delightfully teased his nose.

"I've never been a tea drinker," he said. "It's not strong enough for me."

"Well, at the moment, my stomach feels a bit on the queasy side. Peppermint tea is just the ticket for that."

"Sir, may I get you something?" the flight attendant asked quietly.

"Tonic water, I think."

After a moment, Douglas heard the lid of a can pop, then the fizz of carbonated liquid flowing into a glass. There were few sounds Douglas truly loved. But, this sound, like several others, signaled a memory. He'd loved this sound ever since childhood. It reminded him of his grandfather, a hearty, German man who drank a lot of seltzer.

"It's on the top, left corner of your tray, Sir."

"Thank you."

Douglas would remember the efficiency of this airline. It wasn't everyday employers took pains to teach their staff about the special needs of customers with disabilities.

"Say listen, Doctor, maybe your visit to Chicago

doesn't have to be purely business. There's a lot to see and do in Chicago. Would you care to join me in some sightseeing?"

"That sounds like fun. I'm not sure I'll have much time for relaxation, but if I do, I'd love some company. Could I call you?"

"I'm not carrying a cell phone while on vacation. It's a little harder for my boss to contact me that way. But, I'm staying at the Crowne Plaza, on Wabash Street. You can reach me there."

A rush of happiness washed over him when the woman said she looked forward to seeing him again. It surprised him.

Clearly this vacation would be something special after all.

# CHAPTER THREE

O'Hare International Airport was bigger than JFK and, since far more travelers passed through it each day, Douglas found it difficult to wind his way through the long, crowded hallways without assistance. All around him voices filled the air and the PA system constantly blared announcements. Because he'd forgotten to arrange to be met at the tail end of his trip, and none of the flight crew remembered to ask if he needed help, he struggled with trying to make his way out of the terminal on his own. Every few feet he bumped into an obstacle. Indoors, and still reliant on the sonic cane instead of the navigator, he had no way of knowing what obstacles lay in his path until either he hit it or it hit him.

Finally, after what felt like hours, Douglas managed to get out of the building. Switching off the cane, he put it back in his pocket, and switched on the Navigator. As expected, the device took longer than usual to boot up. According to the company's website, a slight delay could occur whenever the device loaded a new map. The momentary lapse frustrated him.

Suddenly, the world came to life. The beeps of people rushed past him. A nearby street sign called out to him. Vehicles issued warning challenges as they whizzed down the street. Walking to the curb, he raised his arm to hail a cab. A few minutes later, he climbed into a vehicle smelling very much as if an animal died and been burned inside. He found himself hoping all of Chicago wasn't going to be characterized by this particular smell.

"Where to, Buddy?"

"The Crowne Plaza Hotel, please. It's on the corner of Wabash and Madison, I believe."

"Yes, Sir. That's where it is, all right. Nice place. Of course, in my opinion, it's a far cry from the grandeur of the original building, but you'll like it anyway, I'm sure."

Douglas shook his head. "Original building? What do you mean?"

"The one there before the earthquake destroyed it a year ago."

"You mean this isn't the same Crowne Plaza? The historic landmark building?"

"Nope. Sorry to disappoint you. It kind of looks the same, but you can see the differences. They rebuilt it the best they could. I guess they couldn't copy such an old building perfectly. My sister stayed there for her wedding night. She said it was a wonderful place. I'm not a romantic guy myself, but some people are. Whenever a young couple comes to town looking for a place to stay, I recommend the Crowne Plaza. If I see you again while you're in town, you'll have to tell me what you think of it."

"I'm sure I'll enjoy my stay there. Architecture is kind of a hobby of mine. In my opinion, you don't have to be able to see to appreciate the warmth of a building."

"Okay, if you say so."

The cab continued its journey through the streets of the city. Douglas tried in vain to ignore the foulness in the air, covering his nose with his hand. But, tendrils of stench snuck past his fingers. He didn't feel a draft, which meant none of the car's windows were open. The source of the offensive aroma resided inside the vehicle. He couldn't think of a polite way to tell the driver his car stank. Undoubtedly over time the man's nose became desensitized to the smell. And, given his response to Douglas's comment about the warmth of buildings, he thought it best to just keep quiet. By the time the trip ended, half an hour later, he felt like he needed a long, hot shower to get rid of the stench. His increased dependence on smell held both negative and positive aspects.

Douglas hurried into the foyer of the hotel just as a strong, icy wind sent a chill down his spine. Although he had spent only a few minutes in the open air, he felt chilled to the bone. Chicago had a reputation for its long, cold winters. Apparently now, in mid-September, the winter already began. Unfortunately, his thin, blue jacket and black Fedora were all he'd thought to bring along to protect him from the elements during this trip.

Before making any reservation, Douglas researched Chicago's hotels carefully. Although none of them fit all his criteria, the Crowne Plaza came the closest. In the 1800's this building housed the Chicago headquarters for the jewelry and precious metals trade, which he'd taken to mean the architecture was probably exceptionally beautiful, incorporating both high ceilings and large windows. Granted, he wouldn't be able to see these things, but he would be able to feel the brick and terra-cotta composing the building's exterior and run his fingers along the "Arts and Crafts" style decor adorning the interior. It would have to suffice.

This hotel met another of Douglas's needs, a close

proximity to several prominent museums. He particularly wanted to visit the Art Institute of Chicago where this week, as luck would have it, works by one of his favorite artists, Helen Fukuhara, along with other blind artists, would be on display. He'd been a fan of Fukuhara's multi- textured collages even when he could see. Her use of different materials and fabrics fascinated him. Now, as a blind man, he appreciated her work from a completely different perspective, based on his sense of touch and the images his fingers brought to his mind's eye. He only regretted his inability to see the juxtaposition of colors in the various works of art.

Douglas knew a little about Fukuhara's life, and what he knew made him respect her accomplishments. Born blind, she developed an appreciation for music early in life, and honed her appreciation into a talent. As a young girl, Fukuhara's parents and teachers repressed her artistic endeavors, so it wasn't until later in her life, once she determined to pursue her own path despite the opinion of others, that she felt capable of expressing her interest in the visual arts. That same kind of commitment gave Douglas his new lease on life.

* * *

From the airport, Cordelia took a cab to an address on South Wacker Drive where the University of Illinois housed its Cook County office and laboratory. For some reason she still couldn't understand, Joshua insisted she go there before checking into her hotel. Inside the cab, Cordelia listened to the news report playing over the radio.

"In Mexico City yesterday, a crowd numbering no

fewer than ten thousand gathered in the center square to demand the resignation of President Emanuel Hasta. President Hasta is being blamed throughout the country for not doing enough to increase the production of corn, or decrease the price of corn meal.

"According to experts, cornmeal has risen to an all-time high of three dollars per pound. This, combined with a significantly disproportionate rise in the minimum wage, has caused widespread panic and a rash of deaths linked to starvation. For his part, President Hasta blames the United States, from which Mexico receives forty percent of its corn imports. His administration says the United States' refusal to use biomass instead of corn for its ethanol production causes a severe shortage in the amount of corn available for export. The recent epidemic affecting Mexico's corn crop has made a bad situation worse. Agricultural pathologists agree the disease has caused a twenty percent decrease in Mexico's available corn crop over the past three months."

The commentator went on to report although the demonstration began peacefully, when hecklers began questioning Mr. Hasta's policies, the scene quickly became ugly. Within minutes of beginning his speech, they began pelting Hasta with rotten fruit and vegetables, including diseased ears of corn.

"I can't grow enough corn to feed my family, let alone sell," Orlando Hernandez, a corn farmer who traveled seven hours to participate in the demonstration was quoted as saying. "There has to be a way for the government to help the farmer. I came here today to make sure the president shares the responsibility for the lives of my family."

The cab driver, a burly man with a mop of thick, brown

hair, turned off the radio with a shake of his head.

"Can you believe this," he said, in a gravelly, Russian accent. "People are going crazy again. The same thing happened in my country in 2001. People don't understand. A government cannot do much in these situations. President Putin tried, but failed. Mexico's president will fail also."

"That was a potato disease, wasn't it," Cordelia asked. Her gaze shifted upward, attempting, in her mind's eye, to see the facts of that plague among the jumbled pieces of information in her head.

"I'm surprised an American would remember something like that," the driver grumbled, glancing at her by way of the rearview mirror. "Americans don't usually pay attention to things happening outside their own country."

"I'm not a typical American. I'm a plant pathologist. I study diseases affecting crops."

"Very interesting. Then, you know about this corn disease in Mexico? All the poorest people are going to starve, just like they did in my country. Putin tried to hide it from the public, so very few people even know Russia had a potato problem. My cousin Andrey, who works in the Department of Agriculture, told me about it."

"That's what I'm doing here in Chicago, trying to find a cure for the disease."

"I wish you more luck than our scientists had. They only recently discovered the strain of disease that destroyed our potatoes. Of course, now it is too late."

The cab stopped in front of a squat, massive building extending along most of a city block. Cordelia became instantly aware of how drastically seismic activity altered the surrounding area even since her last visit only a month ago. The remnants of a recent earthquake were everywhere. Broken glass littered the street. Uneven concrete slabs made the walkways treacherous. The tops of uprooted white oak trees leaned through several smashed windows. Gingerly, she made her way into the building through a boarded-over door.

A tall, thin man stood in the vestibule. When the door closed, he walked toward her with an outstretched hand, his every step accentuated by the echo of his cane tapping on the marble floor.

"Cara," the man said, his face brightening with recognition. "I'm glad to see you made it back here safely. You've no doubt surmised, I'm sure, you just missed a rather serious earthquake."

"Hello, Eduardo. It seems like I did. Lucky, I guess."

"Fortunately, we were spared most of the effects. There is some turned over furniture and a few pieces of glass broke, but that's all."

"Tell me, why was I told to come directly here instead of going to the hotel from the airport? My assistant was not very clear about that."

"I wanted to see you as soon as you got in. I needed to see your lovely smile, and I couldn't get away to meet you. There's just too much to do before the conference begins. Too many dignitaries to greet. Are you all right? You look a bit green."

Ortega's voice, both warm and inviting, belied eyes which were cold, hard, piercing. Something disturbed her about them, but Cordelia couldn't place it. Her fatigue probably clouded her intuition, she told herself, dismissing the notion.

"It's nice to see you again too, Eduardo. I'm all right. I'm just tired and my stomach is a bit upset, probably from the turbulence on the flight. Frankly, I would have preferred to lie down on a nice, comfortable hotel bed when I got in rather than coming directly here."

"I'm sorry about that. I just wanted to be the first to greet you." He smiled, making the ends of his thin moustache point toward his eyes.

"Have there been any new outbreaks?"

"No, thank Gaia."

*What an odd phrase.*

"Gaia?"

"The Earth Goddess."

Cordelia pursed her lips. She wasn't used to, or comfortable with, a scientist with Ortega's reputation espousing religious ideology. Something else bothered her too. Instinctively, she knew this man would let nothing stand in his way. It worried her.

* * *

"May I help you, Sir?"

The baritone voice addressing him echoed before reaching Douglas's ears. This meant the sound bounced off the lobby's walls and furnishings instead of being absorbed by them.

Introducing himself, Douglas reached into his jacket pocket and pulled out a slip of paper with a series of dots embossed onto it. Slowly he ran the tip of his finger over them. "I'm checking in today. My reservation number is Y12864J."

Blind Traveler's Blues

While he waited for the clerk to confirm his reservation, Douglas listened to the soft, jazzy melody coming from a piano to his left. The instrument sounded slightly off key, but he enjoyed its soulful tones nonetheless. He wondered whether hand or machine lay behind the music. Once he'd settled in, he'd have to find out.

"I'm sorry, Sir. There seems to have been a mix up. We have you listed as checking in tomorrow."

"Tomorrow? But I called yesterday to make sure the reservation was confirmed. I wasn't told of any problems. I'm here today, and I need a room." *This is unbelievable!*

"My sincere apologies, Sir. We only have a small number of accessible rooms, but I'll see what I can do."

When Douglas expounded on how long a day he'd had, and how tired he felt, the clerk assured him a suitable room would probably become available soon.

Douglas listened to the tap-tap-tap of the clerk's footfalls moving away from the counter. Then, using his cane's sonic pulses to guide him, he crossed the lobby to a chair at the bar where he let the piano music wash over him. It would not serve him, he realized, to let his anger get the best of him over something trivial like a messed up reservation. Given time the situation would be resolved.

"Sir, would you care for a drink?" The woman's voice, light and melodious, made a music of its own.

Douglas took his titanium-framed sunglasses off his nose then rubbed his dead eyes with the back of his hand, a reflex action left over from the days when he could still see.

"That might be just what I need. Do you think you could bring me some Amaretto, with a splash of orange juice? The good stuff, Di Saronno, please."

"I'm sure I can get that for you, Sir."

After the waitress walked away, Douglas felt the presence of another person standing before him.

"Sir, we've solved the problem," the desk clerk said. "One of the guests in an accessible room just called to say he was checking out. You can take the room as soon as the housekeeping staff has straightened it out."

"Thank you. I was beginning to think I'd need to find another place to stay."

"No need to worry about that, Sir. We would have found some way to accommodate you. We've never turned away a guest, except while the reconstruction was going on, of course."

"I heard about that. The cab driver told me a little about your earthquake damage on the drive from the airport."

"The quakes are a real problem. About a year ago one of them destroyed the hotel. It's a good thing the government funded the rebuilding."

"They did what?"

Given the extent of recent earthquake damage, an offer of assistance from the government wasn't surprising. But, an offer to do so at no charge to the hotel owners was shocking.

"We became one of the Unimat Corporation's project buildings," the man was saying now. "All very hush-hush. They were looking for testing sites for their new building material, Plasteel. It's supposed to be earthquake-proof. After the quake earlier today, a particularly nasty one I'm glad you missed, I'm a believer.

"At the time we weren't allowed to tell anyone. The staff had to sign all sorts of secrecy forms. Now I suppose it's okay to mention it."

Douglas cringed at hearing the word "Plasteel." The material, a combination of plastic and steel supposedly more resilient to the shockwaves of earthquakes than any other, was the creation of Unimat and John P. Haggarty, and the reason for Haggarty's murder. Douglas had accidentally gotten mixed up in the crime. His friend, Eddie, also became a victim when Haggarty's murderer came gunning for him. To this day, the entire affair still gave him nightmares.

When the waitress returned with his drink, Douglas lifted the glass to his nose, allowing the nutty aroma of the Amaretto to waft into his nostrils before bringing the glass to his lips. He took a long pull, listening to the cubes of ice tinkling and cracking inside the glass. The combined orange juice and almond-flavored liquor bit at his throat, but he relished the taste. In a moment he forgot about the trouble with the reservation. He finally felt like his vacation had really, finally begun.

* * *

After finding a cab for Cordelia, Dr. Eduardo Ortega decided to visit one of the building's five laboratories before continuing his work on the week-long conference. Most of the scientists would not be arriving until the next day, and the last-minute arrangements were virtually complete anyway.

The University of Illinois at Chicago held one of the best agricultural research departments in the United States, with a world-wide reputation for excellence, particularly in the field of emerging pathogens, a fact in which, as administrator of the Cook County facility, the sixty-year-old Ortega took considerable pride in. He personally supervised the discovery of several new species of bacteria.

The previous meetings produced few results. They had, however, allowed the scientists to organize themselves into groups, each attacking the problem from different angles. The woman he just greeted, Doctor Cara Cordelia, led the group charged with identifying the origin of the bacteria.

They all knew the spores came from Mexico, but because they were not of an easily identifiable species, the group did not know how the bacteria came into being. Learning this detail would help the scientists understand how the disease disseminated through the country so rapidly. Because of the symptomology, it seemed possible the disease could be the missing link between several varieties of pathogens, but this hypothesis remained, as of yet, unproven. If it turned out to be true, there very possibly might be a Nobel Prize in the offing because, to Ortega's way of thinking, the disease would change the world.

Leaning heavily on his cane, Ortega entered the laboratory. Crammed into the small, white room were fifteen of the brightest scholars at the university, each of whom had made significant contributions in their separate fields. Now they focused on a single project, one Ortega held especially close to his heart, and he watched them like a hawk would watch over its chicks.

Because, as the infection spread, samples of the first ancient spores to come into contact with present day corn plants became scarcer, most of the scientists examined next-generation spores from newly infected plants, with interesting results. Whether they worked with original or next-generation spores, each of the scientists ran into the same problem. In the early stages of the investigation the collected spores were placed onto Petri dishes containing a nutrient medium, before being incubated. This normally began the process of germination and the formation of identifiable colonies. These spores, however, appeared to be obligate parasites, meaning they wouldn't grow on anything but the host plant. Therefore, the scientists were forced to rely on the more labor-intensive process of studying the spores under a microscope, virtually eliminating any opportunity for this group to study the growth and distribution properties of the disease.

Ortega fixed his attention on Dr. Elizabeth Tuttle, his latest mistress, as the young, red-haired woman peered at the LCD screen of a hand-held, digital microscope. After a moment she looked away briefly to jot down a note, finally squeezing a trigger on the handle of the device, wirelessly uploading an image of whatever she'd been studying to a computer, and shared with off-site researchers. Ortega smiled. These scientists used some of the most cutting-edge equipment in the world, but they were still running out of time.

Before leaving New York, Douglas learned about a famous Blues club, Buddy Guy's Legends, and decided he had to visit.

Born in Louisiana, Guy taught himself to play guitar by the age of thirteen. At twenty-one years old, he moved to Chicago to practice his craft. Douglas respected the discipline it took to learn an instrument without outside instruction. His own goal, teaching himself to play harmonica, often proved to be an exercise in futility.

"Discovered" by Muddy Waters, one of Douglas's

favorite musicians, Guy often played with B.B King, another favorite. The original club opened in 1969, and been rebuilt three times since then. According to the website Douglas read, Buddy Guy's Legends still maintained its original blues-inspired atmosphere and tradition of playing host to some of the biggest names in the music business.

It would be a thrill to step into the establishment, like traveling back to a period in time when the great musicians of the genre were in their heyday. Listening to a band recreate some of his favorite music would, no doubt, be soothing. Douglas picked up the phone. The woman who answered promised him a very relaxed atmosphere, offering sumptuous food, great music, video games, and several regulation-size pool tables. After listening to the tinny voice of his watch call out eight o'clock, very much past his usual dinner time, he rushed downstairs to hail a cab.

Walking through the club's door, Douglas's ears were bombarded by the sound of people screaming at one another in order to be heard over the din, waitresses taking orders, and, to his left, the distinctive clack of pool balls colliding. To his right, a trio of musicians played Delbert McClinton's song, *Monkey Around.*

The sounds from the pool games-it sounded like three distinct games were going on at the moment-brought memories of his childhood when, to his surprise and delight, his parents gave him a pool table for his birthday one year. He quickly learned to love the game, constantly trying out new shots and variations he'd seen on television. When his Aunt Joan and Uncle Lou visited, he would challenge his uncle to a game, making friendly wagers on the outcome. The memory, especially of the last game they played together before a stroke left his uncle unable to speak and barely able to move, tasted bittersweet. Afterward, the game lost much of its allure.

Guided by his cane, though the noise level made paying attention to the device's impulses difficult, Douglas walked into the club, bumping into several tables along the way. Eventually someone, probably a member of the staff, offered his assistance. Douglas switched off the cane and let himself be helped to a table, which, judging by the sound of the band, sat directly in front of, but not terribly close to, the stage.

For the next two hours, Douglas listened to music, drank, and ate a variety of dishes he would never have been tempted by at home, including one of the house specialties, alligator fritters smothered in hot sauce. At one point he even considered pulling out his harmonica and trying to follow along with the music, but quickly dismissed the notion. Strangely, though he rarely felt the need for companionship, feminine or otherwise, his thoughts drifted to Cordelia. He hoped she would find time to get in touch with                                                                 him.

## CHAPTER FOUR
*Day 3*

Douglas began to plan his day while standing in the shower.

*I suppose I should get business out of the way before doing anything else.*

Frowning, he climbed out of the shower, wrapping a towel around his waist before reaching into his wallet for the scrap of embossed paper he'd placed there before leaving the office. After running his finger over the Braille characters, he picked up the phone and felt for the number keys, only to find there weren't any. Instead, through the earpiece, a woman's soft voice asked for the number he wanted.

"I'd like..."

The woman cut him off, sharply repeating her question.

*Hmm, voice activation, probably a limited vocabulary system. Fine.* "847-555-7683"

"Thank you. One moment while I connect you."

The phone rang four times before a man with a heavy Irish brogue answered. Introducing himself, Douglas explained his position with Datascan Corporation, and said his boss, Sid Coltrane, asked him to make contact.

"You don't say. Abledan, is it?" His voice sounded dismissive, impatient.

"Mr. Coltrane did phone to say I was going to call, didn't he?"

"Your man did call. Yes'sir. So, what can I do fir ye, Mr. Abledan?"

"I was told I would be doing something for you. Mr. Coltrane sent me because I'm a software specialist. I find the right tools to do different jobs."

"Oh, yeah. That's what he said a'right. Why don't you come by the place and I'll show ye the problem. Our whole operation is a bit banjaxed right now. We're not getting anything done. Got plans for lunch?"

"As a matter of fact, I haven't."

"That's no good. Come 'round. We'll go to the local, have a pint, and talk over the problem. We're on Washington Street, right near where the Civic Center used to be."

Douglas felt his watch. "I can be there at 2:30, if that's okay for lunch, Mr. ... I didn't get your name."

"Peter Faggan. I'll see ye then, Mr. Abledan."

Douglas finished dressing, and turned to walk out the door, when the phone rang. To his delight, he heard Cara Cordelia's melodious voice greeting him.

"I didn't expect to hear from you so soon, Doctor."

"Please, call me Cara. I have a free morning and thought I would take you up on the offer of sharing a meal."

"That's wonderful! Unfortunately, I have plans for this morning. And, I have an appointment this afternoon; it's that business I told you my boss wanted me to do. In fact I was just heading out the door. Could we meet later, for dinner?"

"I'll have to check my schedule for this evening. You said you like Blues, didn't you? One of my colleagues from New York told me about an old-style blues club here in Chicago, called Capone's. As it happens, it's not too far from your hotel. It's supposedly done up in 1920s style. There are even waitresses dressed as flappers. I can give you a call later."

"Sounds great. I'm looking forward to seeing you."

Douglas hung up the phone and rushed out the door, reflecting on the call. If he did nothing else while in Chicago, having dinner with Cara Cordelia would be enough to make his vacation memorable.

* * *

Almost immediately after Cordelia hung up the phone, the pain in her abdomen returned. She'd been awakened by it last night and taken an antacid, which did nothing to relieve the discomfort. A lunch date with Douglas, she realized, would have been an extremely bad idea after all. Running into the bathroom, she crouched over the toilet, retching until her stomach finally stopped cramping.

*This is what I get for eating food from a street cart.*

Catching a glimpse of herself in the bathroom mirror, her eyes widened in dismay. The color had drained from her skin, and her usually perfectly-coiffed hair draped limply over her face.

Once the pain subsided somewhat, Cordelia stumbled toward her bed. Picking up the phone, her manicured fingers shaking from the effort, she called the front desk. With any luck the hotel could connect her with a doctor.

"I'm sorry you're ill, Doctor," a soft, feminine voice said. "Could it have been something you ate? I hope it's not something we served you."

"Perhaps. I've never had food poisoning before. But no, I didn't eat here. I had something off a cart in Millennium

Park late last night."

"I see. Well, I'll page the doctor and have him come up as soon as he can."

Cordelia laid back on the bed, exhausted and sweating, her head pounding. Her heart raced, but she managed to close her eyes, trying to block out the morning light. Finally, she fell into a fitful sleep, only to be woken by a knock on the door.

Groggy, and with a stomach feeling as if it held a fully expanded balloon, she made her way to the door. She'd been asleep for just over half an hour and now, on top of everything else, every nerve in her body burned as if on fire. Walking the few feet to the door felt like trekking through a lake of molten lava. When she finally reached the portal, she almost collapsed into the arms of a large man with short black hair and a pockmarked face. Under other circumstances she might have been afraid of him, now she just didn't have the strength.

"I'm the hotel physician, Dr. Crane. Here, let's get you back to the bed," he said in a slow, deep voice, prodding her across the room with his hand resting on her shoulder. "I wasn't told your condition was this bad."

"I'm okay, really. It's just my stomach. It started acting up last night. Cramps. I threw up a couple of times. This morning I feel like I'm going to explode and I'm a bit nauseous. The stuff I've been taking isn't helping. I don't like taking medications anyway. They rarely help me, but I'm diabetic so I have to take insulin several times a day."

Crane's hand pressed on Cordelia's forehead, then he took a small, thin probe from his pocket, slowly waving it over her head. When it beeped, he put on a pair of horn--

rimmed glasses, held the device a few inches from his eyes, and strained to read the display.

"Hmm, ninety-nine point eight. Not too bad, but you'd better stay in bed a little while and rest. I'll write a prescription and have it sent up to you. I think you may just have a touch of stomach flu. Not the best way to spend a vacation, is it?"

"I'm not on vacation, Doctor. I'm here in Chicago to attend an agricultural pathology conference which begins tomorrow."

"Well then it's even more important you spend the day resting, so you'll feel well enough to attend your meeting. If you need anything further, have the desk page me, or call my office for an appointment."

Once the doctor left, Cordelia tried unsuccessfully, to sleep. A life-long diabetic, ingrained with the risk of contracting all its potential complications, she'd come to know her body well. She didn't recall ever feeling this horrid. Something was terribly wrong.

* * *

Outside his hotel, the wind kicked up. Pulling his coat more tightly around him, Douglas switched on his navigator, and heard the beeps representing the people and objects around him. In the short time he'd been here, Chicago had taken on a life of its own. In so many ways this city resembled New York; many of the sounds and smells could be found in any big city, but there were differences too. If someone questioned him, he wouldn't have been able to explain it, but even the cars sounded differently than they did in New York.

Since, according to the information he'd found on the Internet before leaving New York, the Art Institute of Chicago lay only a few blocks away, he'd decided he would begin his day there. He walked south down Wabash Avenue to the corner of Monroe Street where, to the right, the Schubert Theater called out its presence in a whisper indicative of its relative distance. He turned left and waited for the tone of the traffic light to signal safe passage across the street.

Around him, between the sounds emitted by the navigator, he heard pieces of conversations. From the little he picked up, it seemed apparent a number of the people around him also planned to visit the museum, and he enjoyed the idea of being in the company of fellow art lovers. Arriving on Michigan Avenue, hearing the museum call out to him, and then climbing its granite staircase, he recalled his many visits to the Metropolitan Museum of Art in New York City.

For the next few hours Douglas wandered through the halls of the museum. Each painting seemed to come to life, its history and imagery unfolding in vivid detail through the wireless headset he'd been given.

Upon entering the building the docent explained he would not need his sonic cane. In fact, the young man said, it would interfere with Douglas's enjoyment of the exhibits. Instead, a silk rope glided through his hand, guiding him from place to place.

Douglas's thoughts wandered back to his childhood, when he'd first been exposed to the art world. Back then, despite the fact his father enjoyed painting, he only cared about the bright colors and interesting shapes. Still, when they visited museums, he listened to the recorded voice on the CD player the museum provided.

Now, years later, two things were different. First, a CD player no longer constrained his movements as he moved about the various works of art. The descriptions now came from a device set into the wall, sensing when a patron stood before a particular exhibit, then beaming an audio description of it to wireless headphones. Second, and much more important, now blind, he could no longer visually appreciate the effort each artist put into his or her work. No longer could he see colors, shapes, or textures. Instead, he relied on his other senses to fill the void.

Fortunately, over the past thirty years, museums expended an increasing amount of time and money to make sure their exhibits were accessible to people with disabilities. At those exhibits where impracticality, for whatever reason, prevented placement of one of these devices, the museums affixed plaques with short descriptions in Braille. The staff at the Campus insisted he learn to read by touch. At the time he thought it a pointless exercise. Now he appreciated the effort.

Douglas rode the elevator down to the building's lower level, to visit both the Touch Gallery and the special exhibit of works by blind artists. He let his fingers roam carefully over the twenty-seven pieces comprising the Gallery's collection, each of which represented a different culture and period in history. One piece, a sculpture by Alison Ulman entitled *Luxury Loft,* depicting a woman sitting on a balcony outside an open window, he examined with particular care. The steel comprising most of the sculpture felt cold against his flesh. The plastic doll, representing a woman, conveyed a loneliness and sadness he could relate to because, in some small way, his blindness, at times, made him feel isolated.

Next down the line he discovered a mixed media sculpture by Lou Giraldi. The wood making up its legs felt warm and craggy, while the papier mache head felt cool, smooth, and damp.

Finally, at the very end of the gallery, Douglas found an untitled collage by Helen Fukuhara. Running his hands over fabrics of different sizes, shapes, and textures, he envisioned a landscape with rolling hills, a place where the upper elevations might be snow-capped.

By the time he left the museum, the temperature plummeted. His thin coat offered little protection, but he didn't care. Exploring the museum, he felt, left him with a life-affirming sensation.

* * *

"Nice to see ye, Mr. Abledan."

Faggan's accent, virtually imperceptible on the phone, but much stronger in person, forced Douglas to listen closely in order to understand any of the man's words.

"Wish I could say the same, Mr. Faggan, but it is nice to hear your voice up close and personal."

"Oh, you're blind ain'tcha? Yeah, your man did mention your 'situation' come to think o' it. If I'd have remembered, I'd have come 'round to see ye. Did ye have any trouble finding the place? We're a wee bit outta the way, we are."

"That's okay, in fact I walked here. This place isn't too far from my hotel and it gave me a chance to test my navigator someplace other than New York City."

"They're kinda spooky if ye ask me."

"Navigators? Most people use some form of navigator these days, don't they?"

"I don't trust the things."

"I'd be lost and helpless without mine. Besides, I love to walk, to get to know my surroundings by the sounds and smells. Chicago isn't as loud a city as New York, and the lake gives it a nice, briny aroma, though not as strong as the ocean. I like it."

"Sounds like you do pretty well fir yourself, being blind and all."

"I haven't always been blind. My condition is due to an accident that occurred two years ago."

"You don't say. I'm sorry. Well, shall we get 'er going? In case your man didn't tell you, you're at the home office of Pembroke Industries. We're a small company. We manufacturer infrared sensor devices, like them one's they use at the Art Institute to tell when someone is standing in front o' a painting or such. Have you been there? You should see the place. It's very interesting. Hmm, is it okay to say that? I know you can't see."

"It's fine. I love museums and visit them often. In fact, I visited the Art Institute this morning. They have a spectacular touch exhibit, a way for blind people like me to experience various forms of art through our hands."

"Ain't that something? Here, why don't we go get something to eat? We can sit and talk about my problem, and you can tell me how Datascan can fix it. I'll give you a tour o' this place after lunch."

Outside, walking down the street, with dead leaves

crunching under each step, Douglas remembered something his therapist at the Campus drummed into him. She said his ears would act like his eyes once did, and she was correct.

One game the patients played, Beep Baseball, a modified version of the game he'd loved in childhood, taught him to distinguish objects from one another, how to know when an object neared him, how far away it was, and from which direction it approached.

Players used a standard softball bat to hit a sixteen-inch ball emitting an audible beep. After hitting the ball, they ran one hundred feet toward the first of two bases, forty-eight inch high pylons which also emitted sound. When any part of his body made contact with the base, the player would be considered "safe."

While the rules of the game were simple, actually playing it proved difficult. After each of the first few games he played, he left the field with bruises, either from being hit by the ball or by slamming into one of the bases because he'd misjudged the distance to it.

All these skills helped him use his new navigator. He still needed a lot of practice before becoming proficient with the device, and there were many close calls in those early days, but the skills he learned at the Campus had helped speed the learning process.

"Hey, do ye like Italian food, Mr. Abledan? There's a great place 'bout a block away. I'm after a bit o' pasta meself."

Inside the restaurant, Douglas's nose became overwhelmed with the combined aromas of garlic and basil. His mouth watered at the thought of his favorite dish, chicken parmesan. In his mind's eye, he saw red and white-checkered tablecloths and candles burning warmly, their wax dripping down over the Chianti bottles into which they'd been set. The place sounded busy. All around him, the sounds of people talking were accentuated now and then by dishes clashing. Periodically a waitress bumped into the back of his chair, quickly apologizing for the accident.

"So, how can Datascan help you, Mr. Faggan?" he asked after the waiter took their orders.

"Well, as I told ye, we make infrared sensor devices. Most of them act like a switch to turn something else on, like the descriptions of objects at the museum. But, the sensors get messed up when they're shaken up too much, and our customers are complainin'. With all the earthquakes the devices keep rebooting."

"That sounds more like a hardware problem, but maybe we can create a software workaround. I'm thinking some kind of stabilization subroutine should help."

"Err, yeah. That should do 'er. How quick can ye do it? We're dyin' here. Can ye start today?"

Douglas shook his head. "I'm sorry. It isn't that easy, and I couldn't start today even if I wanted to. The schematics of your device, and a detailed description of how it's supposed to work, need to be sent to my office for review. The software code needs to be analyzed as well. That's not a one-day, or even a one-man, job. Besides, I'm only meeting with you as a favor to my boss. As I told you, I'm here on vacation."

"I see," Faggan muttered. "Yer one of them guys with a strong work ethic then. Ye work when it's convenient."

"Your sarcasm isn't necessary, or appreciated, Mr. Faggan," Douglas protested. "It's not like that at all. I work hard. I'm very dedicated to my work and my company. I just need time to clear my head. If you knew what I've been through lately you'd understand."

"Oh, I understand a'right. This project ain't important to ye. I'll be giving your man a call, I will. I'll be telling him about this meeting and your attitude."

Douglas could sense his blood pressure rising. "There is no need for that. When I get back to New York, I promise to start on this project. I'll tell my boss it's a top priority. What I need you to do is send the schematics to my office. By the time I get back the hardware guys should have it studied them and I'll be ready to take a look at the software. How's that?"

Sid would be hearing about this.

* * *

Ortega sat in his locked office, staring at the wall, his hands resting behind his head, his feet propped on a stack of papers on his desk. The lights were off, leaving only enough sunlight coming in through the window to give the room an eerie glow in which the framed degrees on the wall gleamed. Back in the days when he was purely a scholar he never imagined himself in the position he now contemplated. Events were not unfolding as expected. Changes were needed, to speed some things up and slow others down. Taking his feet off the desk, he reached for the phone.

"Capone's," he said quietly into the mouthpiece.

The university paid extra to make sure the phone software they ordered recognized more than just numbers, like most others did. Ortega hated having to remember trivial things. He simply led too complex a life. Phone numbers of people and places he called often fit into this category. Most of the things he hated about his current job, revolved around arranging the details associated with things like conferences.

A man with a husky voice answered after five rings. Ortega asked for Lucy Tanner.

"May I tell her who is calling?"

"She'll know."

The phone went silent for the next five minutes. Ortega hated the quiet. He'd prefer to be listening to news, music or even the weather report, anything to keep his mind busy while he waited.

"This is Lucy. Can I help you?"

"This is Ortega."

"Hi, honey. I'm so glad you called. Are you coming to see me tonight?"

The woman had a shrill voice. Ortega despised it.

"No. Listen, I'm sending someone to visit the restaurant this evening, the person I told you about during my last visit. Remember what I said when we discussed this. I've told her to make sure she was seated at your station, and that she'd get the best service."

"I'm not sure I can do this tonight, Eduardo." Her voice became barely audible. Was she having second thoughts about doing his favor? "We were told to expect a very busy night. Some kind of party, I think."

"It has to be tonight. Everything has been arranged already."

"I'll do my best, for you. When can I see you again? It's been so long."

"That's my sweet girl. I'll see you next week."
*Sleep with one of these young girls a couple of times and they become so easy to manipulate.*

* * *

Douglas waited for Cordelia inside Capone's Restaurant. He'd barely had a chance to sit down when he caught a whiff of the perfume she'd worn on the airplane when they'd met.

"It's nice to see you again, Mr. Abledan," she said. "I trust you're all settled into your hotel?"

"It's nice to hear you, Cara." Douglas smiled warmly. "Please, call me Douglas."

Once Cordelia settled into her seat, Douglas asked her to describe the room.

"Imagine going back in time a hundred years. There are Tiffany lamps on each table, giving the room a nice, soft glow. The walls are covered in dark wood panels. And, all along the back wall, is a bar outfitted with an array of bottles of various size and shapes. I wouldn't be surprised if some of them contain bathtub gin."

"It sounds lovely. Now, tell me if I'm right. There's a five-piece band about thirty feet away from our table."

Douglas listened to the music for a few minutes, transfixed by the soulful tone of a saxophone.

"I know this song. It's a Duke Ellington tune. Let me think for a moment. I think it's called *Mood Indigo.*"

"You amaze me, Mr....Douglas. The things you smell. The things you hear. You even recognized the song after hearing only a few notes. I wish my senses were so acute. It would greatly help me in my work."

"My senses are not so much more finely tuned than yours," he told her. "I just have to rely on them differently since I can't use my eyes. Anyway, to answer the question you asked me about my hotel, there was a minor problem with the reservation, but it resolved quickly. They had me scheduled to arrive in town today, not yesterday. How about you? Are you all right?"

"Yes, why do you ask?"

"Something I hear in your voice. I guess you could say I hear a kind of weakness I hadn't heard when we were talking on the plane."

"You do pick up a lot, don't you? I'm fine now, but last night and this morning I was ill with a bad stomachache and slight fever. I even had the hotel call a doctor."

"We could have done this another night, you know."

"No, it's okay. I'm fine now. My stomach is just a bit queasy. I'll just have to watch what I eat tonight."

Douglas didn't like her tone, which wavered slightly, not like someone who felt completely well. She coughed once and the sound seemed "wet," not the kind of dry sounding cough resulting from the cigarette and cigar smoke permeating the air. Footfalls approaching on the carpeted floor distracted him from inquiring further.

"Hello, my name is Lucy." The woman's voice, high-pitched and squeaky, sounded more like a girl's than a woman's. "I'll be your server tonight."

"I love the color of your dress," exclaimed Cordelia. "It's such a lovely shade of red. Douglas, I wish you could see it. It's just beautiful. But don't those beads get in the way when you're serving customers?"

"Thank you, honey. No, the beads don't bother me at

all, and they really make the outfit work."

Douglas nodded. "That explains the clatter I heard as you walked to our table."

"Wow, you've got good ears. You could hear me coming even through all the noise? The dress is full of sequins and beads. The style of the time, I guess. Now, may I get you something to drink?"

"Drink?" Douglas's eyebrow rose. "I thought this was a 1920's club. I'm not up on my history, but wasn't that the time of prohibition?"

"Shh." The waitress's voice dropped to a whisper. "We aren't really supposed to be serving alcohol, but what the feds don't know, ya know. At least we haven't been raided yet."

"Play along, Douglas," Cordelia interjected in a whisper. "I should have told you ahead of time, this restaurant is modeled after the speakeasies of the period. I read a lot about them."

"I see. That accounts for the cigarette smoke as well, I suppose?"

"Yes, Sir. We got special permission from the City Council. The owner argued smoking would add to the 'period' of the place. Personally, I hate it. But, this job pays the bills."

*Sid would love this place.*

Douglas nodded. "Cara, what do you recommend we drink?"

"Well, I'm not supposed to drink. Doctor's orders. But, having just one shouldn't hurt. Besides, I like Old Fashioneds. They're sweet, not too strong, and I think they were popular during the period."

"Excellent idea. We'll both have Old Fashioneds."

"I'll get your drinks right away. Would you care to order your dinner, or would you prefer to wait?"

Douglas ran his finger down the menu. "Hmm. Cara, would you mind ordering for both of us? It appears Braille wasn't very popular in the 1920s."

"No, I suppose not. Today we live in a very open-minded society. Back then, however, people thought those with a disability needed to be taken care of, and, mostly they stayed at home. There were no accommodations made for people like you."

*Open-minded? Not as much as you think.*

Even today, in the 21st century, Douglas frequently faced ingrained societal prejudice. Too many institutions and businesses still failed to cater to the needs of people with disabilities.

"Are you a meat eater, Douglas? I'm in the mood for a thick steak, smothered in onions and mushrooms."

"Sounds great. I haven't had a good steak in a long time. Make mine medium-well, please."

"Excellent choice," the waitress chimed in. "The chef does magic with steak. I'll bring out your drinks. Just sit back, relax, and listen to the show until your dinner is ready."

Once their meals were set before them, Douglas realized just how hungry he'd been. The rumblings of his stomach, aroused by the aromas of onions and garlic, toyed with his senses and seemed to be synchronized to the harmonica music now coming from the stage. He hummed the tune between forkfuls of food.

"I'm afraid I'm not very good company tonight,"

Cordelia said.

"Nonsense, dear lady, you're a charming companion, and a perfect accompaniment to these surroundings."

He had noticed however, Cordelia became quieter during the course of the evening. Clearly something troubled her, but he hadn't thought it appropriate to mention.

"I'm afraid I'm not feeling terribly well. Would you mind excusing me for a few minutes while I find a restroom?"

"No, of course not. If you're feeling ill, perhaps we should leave?"

"No, I don't think that will be necessary."

Before Douglas had a chance to respond, he heard hurried footfalls moving unevenly away from the table, and realized the woman struggled to stay on her feet. When she finally returned, just as he contemplated ways to check on her well-being, Cordelia told him she'd become ill while in the restroom. She'd checked her blood sugar level and found it lower than she'd expected it to be, considering they'd just eaten.

"I'm sorry, Douglas, but do you mind if we cut this evening short? I'm really not feeling very well."

"If you aren't well that takes precedent over anything else. Of course we should go. I'm sure there will be other opportunities to get together while we are both in Chicago. Should I accompany you back to your hotel?"

"No, thank you. You're truly a gentleman, but I think I can manage on my own. I've enjoyed your company, and would like to see you again, if time permits while we are both still in town."

After a moment, Cordelia pushed a scrap of paper into

Douglas's hand.

"You'll have to get someone to read this to you. Please, call me in the morning."
Outside, before climbing into a waiting cab, Cordelia kissed Douglas's cheek.

# CHAPTER FIVE
*Day 4*


Douglas woke to the annoying jingle of the phone ringing. After his fingers fumbled on the nightstand for a moment, he picked up the receiver. For the next minute someone coughed into his ear. Normally he would have hung up, but this cough sounded familiar. It was the same gut-wrenching, nauseating cough he'd been hearing for the last two years.

"Doug," Sid wheezed, "you left us in a really bad state here, you know. I sent you there..."

Douglas struggled past the morning grogginess he always felt until he found his voice.

"Sid? I didn't expect to hear from you. No matter. Need I remind you, you didn't send me here? This is my vacation."

"You know what I mean. I gave you an assignment to help a client, a client whom, I don't mind telling you, is plenty angry. I just got off the phone with him. He was rather upset, to put it mildly, with the way your meeting went. He was ranting, and saying you told him his project wasn't important, that you'll get to it when you see fit."

Douglas wasn't surprised Faggan made the call. In fact, he would have been more surprised if he didn't go through with his threat, given his attitude. But, the lack of trust Sid, both his boss and his friend, seemed to be expressing annoyed him.

"You know me better. I'd never treat a client disrespectfully. The guy wanted me to start work on the project right away. I simply told him I couldn't, because I'm on vacation."

"Would it have killed you to do as he asked? Would it have been so bad? We're talking business, and I told you how badly Datascan is doing right now."

Shaking his head, Douglas propped himself up on his pillow.

"You've got to be kidding. This is my vacation. How often do I take vacation time? Besides, I told him to send his device to the office so the tech guys could take it apart, then I'd study it, and the schematics, the minute I got back. That didn't satisfy him, though. He lost his temper, told me I have a bad work ethic, and demanded I get started right away. I explained I wasn't going to do as he commanded. He didn't like my answer, and said he planned to give you a call."

"Actually, he's called several times. He's been looking for you. I told him you were still in Chicago and will get back here soon. He wanted to know how to contact you. I told him he couldn't."

*That's all I would have needed.* "Thank you, Sid."

"He wants you to get right on this project. Doug, he's an important client. And, to be honest, the company really could use his money."

"Sid, I'm here for two weeks. I'll get to it as soon as I get back. You know I will. If the guy calls again just explain that to him."

"Sorry, Doug. I should have done that in the first place. He caught me off guard."

"Well, that should have told you something right there.

I'm one of your best men. How many people complain about my work?"

"No one has, not in the time you and I have been working together."

"Exactly. Anyway, I'll see you in two weeks. Take care."

Before replacing the phone in the cradle, Douglas instructed the mechanized voice to dial the number Cordelia gave him. When she didn't answer, he left a voicemail message asking her to call back.

*I hope that's a sign she's feeling better.*

He finished dressing, then headed out the door. Though concerned about Cordelia's health, Douglas felt more alive than he had in a very long time. He hadn't even had a nightmare last night, surely a positive sign. It wasn't easy for him to socialize, but for some reason he didn't feel like he needed to be guarded with this woman. He hadn't dated since his accident, and rarely met anyone who interested him in the way this woman did. The next time they were together he'd ask her what she looked like.

Minute details weren't very important to him, but he liked to "see" the faces of people he spoke with. Disembodied voices, even those on the telephone, bothered him. Cordelia's voice, though, caressed his ear. From the first moment he'd heard it on the plane, Douglas found himself wanting to hear more. It wasn't just her accent, though he found it alluring. An intelligence and worldliness accentuated her words in a rare and beautiful way. The more he thought about her, the more he hoped their relationship would blossom into something just as lovely.

Blind Traveler's Blues

* * *

Douglas wanted to spend a few hours walking around the city, eventually stopping at the Chicago Tribune building on Michigan Avenue, but the weather didn't seem likely to cooperate. A light rain began to fall just as the door to the hotel closed behind him. He could still explore, but traveling from one place to another would have to be by cab rather than foot. He remembered his first cab experience upon arriving in Chicago, dreading a repeat of it. Before getting into any cab he'd have to remember to take a sniff of the air inside to make sure his nose would survive the trip. In fact, it probably made more sense to take one of the driverless cabs, since they automatically fumigated themselves after a predetermined number of occupants. He walked to the curb, raised his arm into the air, and waited. The raindrops felt like pinpricks of ice pelting his thin jacket.

* * *

Half a block down the road a yellow Dodge Emporium sat by the curb; its sensors scanning the surrounding area. People scurried all around it, but it paid no attention. Suddenly the onboard computer registered a familiar pattern, someone standing by the curb with his arm stretched out toward the road. The electronic brain started the car's engine while considering the traffic pattern of vehicles on the road. Finally, it inserted itself into the flow, adjusting its course and speed to arrive at the waiting human quickly and safely.

* * *

After what felt like hours, a car stopped. Its horn honked. Its door opened. Douglas took a sniff of the air inside, then said hello to a driver who, because of the way the vehicle reacted, he knew wasn't there. He climbed in.

Douglas couldn't wait to touch the Tribune building. To him, the gothic-style structure represented an architecture lover's dream. Over one hundred years old, the building had once won an award for being the most beautiful office building in the world. While he would not be able to see the flying buttresses, he knew they would be there. Making the building even more interesting, especially to a blind person, were the artifacts. Over one hundred and twenty stones and other objects, from famous sites and structures all over the world, were embedded in its base. Through his fingers he'd be able to "see" all those places without having to travel to them.

At less than a mile away, the ride to the Tribune building should have been little more than a puddle jump, but it wasn't. The trip down Michigan Avenue, with its noise, bumps, and odors offended each of his remaining senses. Douglas's head bounced off the roof of the car more than once, particularly when it was bumped by vehicles obviously so old they were not equipped with navigator devices. He'd run across a few of those in New York. In fact one or two narrowly escaped running over him.

When the car finally stopped, and the engine turned off, Douglas paid for the ride by placing his thumb in a slot on the inside of the door. Switching on his navigator, he climbed out of the car, and stepped squarely into a puddle, soaking his shoes in its frigid water.

*Perfect!*

Through his earphones, he heard the Tribune Building call out to him, and he walked toward the sound. Many other people, including a boy on a skateboard he swerved to avoid hitting, apparently had the same idea.

"Sorry, Mister," said a hurried, young voice. "Didn't see you."

"That makes two of us."

Finally, when he reached the old building, Douglas reached out to touch the granite wall. Its surface felt cool, hard, and rough beneath his fingers. Tracing the engraving in the cornerstone, he savored the thrill of touching a piece of history.

In its time, the Chicago Tribune had been the country's most respected newspaper. Now, in an age when the news was delivered electronically, the building stood as a relic of what his friend, Eddie Hatch, called "a simpler time," a remark to which Douglas always responded by saying the past may have been simpler, but not necessarily better.

A musky scent moving in his direction tugged him away from his thoughts.

"Excuse me, Miss, could you please help me find some of the objects incorporated into the building?"

"I'm sorry," a woman responded. "I'm not quite sure what you mean. Can I help you do what?"

"I apologize for disturbing you, but, if it's not too much trouble, I could use some assistance. I'm blind, you see. I know the Tribune building is famous for having incorporated into its fa9ade many objects from buildings around the world. I'd like to "see" them, but I can't seem to find them."

"Oh, now I understand. Sure, I can help. You're not too far away from where you want to be. Let me show you."

She took his hand in hers, sliding it along the wall. One of the stones jutted out a few inches forming a convex surface. Below it, the words "Edinburgh Castle, Scotland" were engraved.

"Thank you for showing this to me."

"You're welcome. You're in the right area now, and there are a lot of other artifacts in the wall. I'll leave you to discover them for yourself. I've got to get going. I'm late for an appointment."

Douglas spent the next hour letting his fingers dance over the surface of the building. From his research he knew one of the bricks held a piece of pipe from the World Trade Center, and he thought he'd prepared himself to find it. But, when his fingers touched it, they froze. A tear rolled down his cheek.

He remembered the day, twenty years earlier, when terrorists attacked New York City, murdering thousands of innocent people. He had been twenty-five years old, and working a block away at his first real accounting job, when someone yelled about a plane going down in the middle of the city. He had run to the window and watched a second plane race through the sky before finally slamming into the tower.

At the moment of impact, Douglas had not been aware of the personal ramifications of the attack. But, to his horror, he soon learned. His old friend, Girard, a lawyer who worked nearby, became one of the casualties, one of the rescuers who died in the aftermath of the attack. Girard, an off-duty fireman, ran in to try to help when the planes hit.

Workers never recovered his body, though several years later his wristwatch was unearthed from the rubble. In his mind's eye, Douglas saw the planes again and heard the horrific boom following the impact when they hit their target. He saw the plume of smoke in the distance rising in the sky.

As if on cue, the stone he rested his hands on vibrated, and the ground began to shake. An earthquake; and it felt like a bad one. All around him, panicked people shouted and scrambled for shelter. In New York he would have fled either into the "padded cell" assigned to him near his apartment. Or, if he'd been caught away from his assigned shelter, he'd get to one of those available to the general public. But, he'd neglected to study how the system worked in this city.

The shelters people dubbed "padded cells" were an amazing feat of engineering-large pits dug deep under the surface of the earth where, inside, reinforced concrete slabs held back the shifting soil and rock. A series of springs attached those slabs to thick walls of shock-absorbing metal alloy, which came together to form a room where people could ride out even the most intense quakes with minimal discomfort. A device on the door checked the identities of people through the tones of the navigation devices they carried.

"Hey, Mister."

Douglas recognized the voice; the woman who helped him earlier.

"You really shouldn't be standing there while a quake is starting. You need help getting to a shelter?"

"I'm not a resident of Chicago. I don't know what I'm

supposed to do."

"You're supposed to get to a cell and wait it out. Don't they teach you anything about safety in New York? Now come on."

"How did you know I am from New York?"

"The accent is unmistakable."

"My dear woman, I don't have a New York accent."

"You're kidding, right?"

Now was not the time to argue. Now was the time to run for his life, and he did.

* * *

The phone rang three times before Ortega decided to answer it. The day wasn't going very well. It wasn't even noon yet, and there had been another earthquake. Despite that, the scientists all arrived safely. He almost wished they hadn't. Though the conference just began, many of them already squabbled, in several different languages, like children. The combination of the two events gave him such a terrible headache he decided to retreat to the solitude of his office. However, he'd forgotten to unplug the phone and, somehow the service had not been disrupted by the quake.

"Hi, honey."

Ortega grunted. "Who is this?"

"It's me, silly, Lucy," the woman crowed.

"What can I do for you?"

"Now, is that any way to talk to the woman you love?"

"I'm sorry. I have a headache."

"Oh, my poor dear. Is it because of the earthquake? I get them sometimes after the earthquakes too. Is there anything I can do for you?"

"Tell me about last night. Did my friend show up and did you do as I asked?"

"Yes, honey. Your friend showed up, with a boyfriend. They seemed very cozy together. Kind of like you and me on our first date." She giggled. "Anyway, she seemed like a nice person. Not every woman would feel comfortable dating a blind man."

"The guy was blind?"

Ortega thought for a moment, trying to come up with the identity of who it might have been. To his knowledge Cordelia had no friends in Chicago.

"Did they sit at your station? Did you hear what they were talking about?"

"They did, but I didn't hear what they were talking about. I didn't really listen though. My Momma taught me it wasn't nice to listen to someone else's conversation. I mean, how would you have felt if someone had listened to us when we were alone?"

Ortega let out a deep, long breath. If he hadn't needed her to do this job, he could easily have taken pleasure in strangling her.

"But, you did do what I asked, didn't you?"

"You mean put something in your friend's drink? You're lucky they both ordered Old Fashioneds. They're very sweet. I mixed the stuff you gave me into hers. Honey, are you sure it was okay? I mean, after she drank it she ran to the bathroom. You know, honey, I can't see the humor."

Ortega's lips curled. "Don't worry about it. It wasn't anything bad, just a joke. She'll be fine. I have to go now. My head is pounding."

"My poor baby. I'll call to check on you later. I hope you feel better, darling."

Ortega hung up the phone, leaned back in his chair, and closed his eyes. Perhaps it wasn't going to be a bad day after all.

* * *

After the quake, Douglas hurried back to his hotel, his heart racing, his forehead damp with perspiration. Living in New York, where quakes occurred daily, he thought he'd been numbed to their danger. But, running for shelter in unfamiliar territory awakened his anxiety. He was exhausted. He'd been looking for an excuse to push him back into a dojo. This seemed to be just what he needed. Before leaving New York he'd searched the Internet for a judo studio in Chicago. The search produced several hits, but only one of them, the Blue Dragon Judo Academy, mentioned working with blind martial artists.

Training in judo proved both difficult and tiring, but Douglas loved it. He'd been introduced to the martial arts at the Campus and found, at least for the short time he worked out, it took his mind off how dramatically changed his life had become. Over the past two years, through many hours of intense study, he'd worked his way up to the rank of *Yonkyu,* Green Belt. Becoming more aware of his body, and learning how to listen to the world, he'd developed a keen sense of events happening around him.

Douglas's instructor taught him the best ways to grab an opponent and throw him off balance, a skill which came in handy both times someone tried to mug him. Whenever he wanted to teach a particular movement, he would tell

Douglas to get into a position where he could touch his opponent's hips, feet, head, legs, and torso. Douglas likened it to the story of the four blind men trying to describe what an elephant looked like by taking hold of different parts of the animal. Fortunately, over time, he learned to be a bit more accurate.

From the very beginning of his study, Douglas learned that, for a blind person, judo offered an advantage over other martial arts primarily because, as a form of wrestling, participants were almost constantly touching. When he trained on perfecting a particular movement, he never needed to "find" his opponent.

Douglas also appreciated the social aspect of his studies. Living in darkness for the past two years both isolated and insulated him. For most of his life he relished in all things visual. Vision allowed for interaction. If he saw someone or something interesting, he interacted with that person or thing. After the shooting, he needed to discover other ways of making an initial contact. Being part of a dojo focused on bringing blind people together fostered camaraderie. The other student's experiences mirrored his own, allowing him to become involved with them in a way he thought lost to him. Over time, he learned the rules of blind etiquette, which helped him not only inside the dojo but outside, in the sighted world, too.

There were, of course, those able-bodied people who did not understand why a blind man, or anyone with a disability for that matter, would study martial arts. In fact, over the years several well-meaning souls discouraged Douglas, suggesting he take up a "safer" hobby. These well-wishers never tired of reminding him the martial arts were, after all, a dangerous undertaking. They said people with disabilities were more "fragile," more apt to be injured trying to practice one of these art forms. Only foolishness, they'd continue to argue, compelled a man to compound a major life challenge with the probability of serious injury.

Douglas thumbed through his wallet until he found the right slip of embossed paper. After reading the numbers with his fingertips, he picked up the phone and repeated them into the mouthpiece. He told the woman who finally answered he was a blind *Yonkyu* visiting Chicago for a short time, and he asked if it were possible to work out in the dojo. She invited him to attend the Green Belt class, which would meet the following evening at eight o'clock.

After hanging up, Douglas realized the work out would not only relieve the tension he'd felt since the earthquake, but would also take his mind off his guilt of leaving Cordelia alone when she'd taken so suddenly ill. When he'd tried to call her the next morning, and received no answer, he'd rationalized she must have been feeling better, but knew he'd continue to worry until he connected with her.

* * *

Above the door to the conference room at the University of Illinois's Cook County facility hung a fire marshal's notice. This room, it read, could hold a maximum of one hundred and fifty people. Today, however, the capacity would be challenged. Scientists from all across North America filed in for the first day of this third conference to discuss how to deal with the rapidly spreading corn disease.

Cordelia stood off to the side of the room, away from most of her colleagues. She was having a hard time concentrating this morning, and the level of chatter wasn't helping. Her stomach pains and fever returned overnight, and now a series of spasms traversed the right side of her body. Before leaving her room, she'd checked her blood sugar level and, finding it much higher than usual for this early in the day, gave herself an injection of Insulin. The medication should have corrected the imbalance and made her feel better. It didn't. But, she couldn't dwell on the problem any further right now. She came to Chicago for the express purpose of meeting with her fellow scientists and speaking at this conference, and she was determined to do so. The work of the other scientists depended on her. Quietly she skimmed through her notes.

Ortega concluded his opening remarks and motioned for her to come to the podium. It took a moment for her to get her leg to cooperate. When it did, she stumbled twice before reaching Ortega's side. From all around she heard the researchers whispering, no doubt wondering whether she was drunk. Even worse, when she'd arrived at the podium and opened her mouth to speak, the words wouldn't come. Reaching for her papers, she lost control of her hands. The sheets floated, seemingly in slow motion, to the thickly carpeted floor. Her head pounding, her heart beating like a kettledrum in her ears, and gripped by violent convulsions, she fell to the floor. Finally, everything went dark.

# Blind Traveler's Blues

# PART TWO
Unsettling Developments

# CHAPTER SIX
*Day 5*

Since Lucy didn't have to be at Capone's until late in the afternoon, she decided to surprise Ortega with a visit. He'd promised to visit her at the restaurant, but he'd made promises before and never kept them. She didn't like men who lied. So many did. But, knowing how busy he was, she wanted to forgive him. She'd make breakfast for him, and they'd talk about their future together. Her heart raced at the thought.

She dressed quickly, making sure to wear the blue, low-cut blouse he liked so much and a pair of tight-fitting, curve-hugging black jeans. Finally, she hung a pair of silver chandelier earrings on her ears. She loved the tinkling sound they made when he kissed her ears.

After searching frantically for her car keys, she rushed out the door. Traffic would be bad this time of the morning. She hoped to reach Ortega before he left for work. With any luck there would be time after breakfast for lovemaking.

*There's no better way to start the day.*

* * *

Douglas woke from a deep, dreamless sleep to the sound of a radio announcer reporting on the earthquake from the day before. Given the current state of the world, such morning reports were common. But, when he heard the reporter mention the Tribune building, his ears perked up.

"Completed in 1925, the structure was not only a feat of architectural genius, but also an international treasure. Nowhere else could visitors come to see a collection of masonry and artifacts taken from monuments all over the world. Now it's all gone, another victim of Mother Nature's temperament."

Douglas's jaw dropped. The Tribune Building gone? He had just been there. After living through many earthquakes in New York City over the past several years he'd seen his share of fallen buildings and he knew this city too would recover. The newscaster continued his report, and the next story shook Douglas's world.

"The start of a conference of world-renowned agricultural researchers at the University of Illinois was delayed today due to the death of one of the group's key members. According to its organizer, Eduardo Ortega, the police are investigating the death of Doctor Cara Cordelia, who died just as she was about to give the conference's keynote address. So far the cause of death has not been determined."

Douglas's heart skipped a beat. He only met Cordelia a couple of times, but he liked her from the start, and looked forward to knowing her better. Now he would not get the chance, and he wanted to know why. The woman seemed healthy enough, despite her dizziness and stomach pains in the restaurant. People her age didn't usually die from these kinds of symptoms. Something felt wrong. He wondered if he could find out more. He wasn't family, not even really a friend.

*There must be a way.*

Douglas sat on his bed, brooding. For the first time since he'd learned about his lost eyesight he found himself on the verge of weeping. He couldn't fathom a reason for Cordelia's death to hit him this hard, but it did. He reached for his harmonica and began to play, hoping the soulful music would calm him, but it didn't. After a moment of thought, he placed the instrument back in its protective sack.

Finally he walked to the closet to find clothes. His fingers panned over the fabrics, deftly reading embossed tags identifying each article's characteristics. Carefully laying out his selection, he walked to the bathroom to shower and shave, something the occupational therapists at the Campus taught him how to do. The two-handed, maddeningly slow, process involved using his left hand as a guide, searching for whiskers, while his right hand trailed closely behind with the razor. Over time he became skilled enough he rarely nicked the delicate skin of his face. Today became one of those rare days. His hand, shaking ever so slightly, allowed the blade to bite into his flesh twice. He dropped the blade and rushed from the room. He simply had to know the truth.

* * *

Lucy's heart beat rapidly with anticipation, until Ortega's door opened and she saw the woman wrapped in her boyfriend's favorite blue towel, the one she usually wore. Her eyes bugged out. The bags of groceries she'd brought slipped from her frozen fingers.

"Who are you?"

"You come to my door and ask who I am? You're

kidding, right? Shouldn't I be asking the questions?"

"This is my boyfriend's apartment. Ernesto Ortega."

Suddenly, a movement inside the apartment caught Lucy's attention. Ortega strode out of the bedroom, his only garment a towel wrapped around his hips. With tears flooding her eyes, she slapped the half-naked woman, and ran down the hall.

"What's going on here, 'Nesto? Who was that woman? Why did she call you her boyfriend?"

"Calm down, Elizabeth. Let me put some clothes on and I'll explain."

"Who the hell was she, Ernesto?" Tuttle shoved Ortega backward into the bedroom, slammed the door behind her, baring Ortega's path.

"All right. If, you must know, she is someone I used to know. I'd hoped she'd stopped coming around by now."

"I'm waiting for an answer, and you're not getting into your clothes until I get one. This is not the time for you to act cute."

Ortega sighed. "Fine. Her name is Lucy. She is a waitress at Capone's. About six months ago we had a brief fling. It was nothing. Now she won't let go."

Tuttle thought for a long, silent moment, before crossing the room and wrapping her arms around Ortega's neck.

"I can understand how she feels. You know, I'll never let you go."

The terrycloth towel slipped to the floor. Ortega cringed. The odor of Pennyroyal, still permeating the woman's hair, stung his nose. One way or another, the women he'd been forced to depend on to complete his plans were becoming more trouble than they were worth. He had to remind himself his relationship with this woman, at least, wouldn't go on much longer.

"It's nothing to worry about, Elizabeth."

* * *

The scene at the laboratory was chaotic. The staff and visiting dignitaries were trained to deal with the illness and death of a plant. But, the sudden death of a colleague was another matter altogether. There were no set procedures for the scientists to follow.

Cordelia's body had been moved to one of the adjoining labs. Tape cordoned off the area. A young African-American man busily took pictures from various angles around the podium. Police officers were in the process of questioning everyone whether they were participating in the conference or not. Following Ortega's suggestion, most of the scientists adjourned to other rooms. A few were hanging around the doorway to the conference room, hoping to be among the first to learn what happened. Ortega himself went back to his office, where he sat with the lights turned off, until a knock came on the door.

"It's open."

A husky man with short black hair and a neatly trimmed goatee entered the dark room and reached for the light switch.

"Please don't do that. I like it dark in here when I'm thinking. Give it a minute. Your eyes will adjust."

Squinting, the man quickly surveyed the room.

"Ah, there you are. I'm Detective Paul Harris, of the

Chicago PD. Can I assume you are Dr. Eduardo Ortega?"

"Since this is Dr. Ortega's office, and he doesn't allow anyone else to use it, we can consider your assumption to be correct. What can I do for you, Detective?"

"My officers are interviewing the members of your staff, but I wanted to talk to you personally about what happened here."

"You mean the sudden death of Dr. Cordelia, of course. You can speak more plainly, Detective. I don't get upset as easily as some of the others do. Death is part of life. We all will die eventually."

"Yes, Sir, but we all don't die for no apparent reason just when we are about to give a lecture, do we?"

"No, of course not. But it's your job to find out why it happened, isn't it?"

"That is what I am trying to do. Can I assume, from your informality, you knew Dr. Cordelia personally?"

"Not really, but I did admire her. An exceptional woman. Beautiful and highly intelligent. This may sound a bit sexist, but beauty and brains are a rare combination in the scientific community. I imagined the possibility of dating her at one point but, for professional reasons, it never would have worked out."

"I wouldn't know about that, Doctor. I'm a cop. I don't travel in the same circles you do."

"Of course."

The corner of Harris's mouth twitched. The degree of this man's pomposity astounded him.

"What can you tell me about Dr. Cordelia? Was she a private person? Did she talk much about herself?"

"We only had a few brief conversations. I've rarely met

a friendlier woman. More outgoing than I would have expected from all I have read about her and her work."

"Her work. Let's talk about that. The conference you were holding here was for agricultural pathologists, wasn't it? Can you tell me what it was all about? I don't know anything about the field."

"Obviously."

Harris clenched his teeth.

"Cara, I mean, Dr. Cordelia, was one of the world's top agricultural pathologists. She specialized in identifying new diseases with the potential of harming agricultural production."

"I see. So the lecture she was to give today was about that? I read somewhere there is a new disease threatening corn, didn't I?"

"Ah, so you do keep up on current events. Excellent. You are correct, Detective."

Harris squeezed his hands into tight balls, then slowly relaxed his grip.

"It's my job to pay attention to things around me. Speaking of which, do you mind if I record our conversation, Doctor? I don't want to miss anything and the recording will help with my investigation."

Without waiting for a response, Harris pulled a digital recorder from his pocket. Looking back at Ortega, he switched it on.

"Very well. As I was about to say, Detective, we were gathered here to discuss a solution to that particular dilemma. You may not know it, but corn is one of the most important of the staple crops, and one of the most ancient."

"I'm not a fan of corn. Never got used to the taste, a bit

too sweet for my palette I guess."

Ortega cleared his throat.

"Despite your palette's objections, most people and animals eat corn. Also, corn by-products are found in many consumer products, from toothpaste to sparkplugs to fuel. Corn is processed into starch, oil, sweeteners, feed products, organic acids, polyols, and a host of other bioproducts. Tens of thousands of people are employed in corn-related jobs. These are only a few of the reasons why the problem of this new disease is so important. The loss of Dr. Cordelia will make our efforts at finding a cure for the new disease much harder."

Harris's eyes began to glaze over, so he took the interview in a new direction.

"Did Dr. Cordelia have any friends or relatives locally? Someone I can contact?"

Ortega pondered the question before answering. Any mention of the "boyfriend" Lucy saw Cordelia with at the restaurant might cause additional, unforeseen complications. Finally, he decided on a course of action, one geared toward sending the cop in a different direction.

"I don't think she did. Of course, I only knew her professionally, so I may not be the best person to answer your question. She came from New York, Cornell University, if memory serves me. You might want to try to reach someone there to get more information. Of course, you can also ask my staff and the other attendees if they know more about her personal life."

"Thank you. I'll be sure to follow up on both of those suggestions. Can you give me the phone number of someone to contact at Cornell?"

"My secretary can do so, I'm sure."

"Well," Harris said flipping off the recorder and returning it to his pocket, "I won't take up any more of your time. Thank you."

"Will we be able to continue our conference, or will the area remain cordoned off?"

"From an official standpoint, I see no reason why you can't continue with your meeting, once the officers have finished examining the area where Dr. Cordelia collapsed. On a personal note, however, you may want to give the staff and guests some time to digest what has just occurred."

"This is what I was considering when you walked in, Detective. I have to weigh the importance of our work with the emotional impact of the immediate situation."

When Ortega spun his chair to face the window, Harris realized he'd been dismissed, but he paused at the door.

"Oh, one more question, if you don't mind."

Ortega turned once again, this time with a scowl stretched across his face which caused his moustache to twitch. The screech of the chair's unoiled springs seemed to accentuate its occupant's displeasure.

"Yes, Detective?"

"Had Dr. Cordelia complained of feeling ill?"

"Not to my knowledge, not to me or anyone else."

Ortega turned his chair toward the window again. It seemed he believed there was nothing more to say on the subject of Cara Cordelia. Harris was not so sure.

* * *

When Harris walked back into the conference room, he

noticed a uniformed officer he did not recognize take something from the lectern and place it into an evidence bag.

"Find something interesting?"

"Nothing exciting. Just a wristwatch. I assumed it belonged to the victim, so I thought it might be something to look at."

"I doubt we'll get anything useful from a watch, but bag and tag it anyway."

"Already done, Sir."

"Did you find anything else that might be useful?"

"No, but no one has examined the body yet, and as far as I can tell only a few of the people in attendance noticed anything odd or out of place. A couple of them said she seemed unsteady on her feet, maybe even a bit tipsy."

"Tipsy, huh? Maybe, but I doubt it. Anyway, the autopsy will tell us. Finish the interviews and let's pack it up. These people have things to do and we're just in the way. Make sure all the paperwork is done before we leave."

*Something tells me we'll be back, though.*

* * *

During the cab ride to the police station on South Lowe Avenue, Douglas tried to decide how he would go about acquiring information about Cordelia's death. He did not like the idea of making up a story or lying. In his experience, lying required a great deal of imagination, courage, and a good memory. Liars needed to remember the lie so they could constantly and consistently update their story.

He remembered the last time he told a lie about anything. He was thirteen years old and playing in the basement of the house he'd grown up in, something he wasn't supposed to do. Reaching to take something off a metal shelving unit, he'd lost his balance, sending a glass bowl crashing to the cement floor. When, from the next room, he was asked about the noise, he lied and said nothing happened. Later, upon discovering the truth, his father punished him, refusing to take him to a Little League awards banquet. He was devastated.

Douglas thought about the time he'd shared with Cordelia. On both occasions she had been charming, bright, and lively. More importantly, she'd made him feel good about himself in a way no other women had since his accident. Given time, he felt sure, they would have formed a steady relationship. He smiled. If he were to start to seriously date anyone it would shock many of his friends and family members. Finally, he decided a bit of extrapolation wasn't a lie, not exactly anyway. He would tell the police, and anyone else asking about their relationship, Cordelia had been his girlfriend. The statement would be enough, he hoped, to ease suspicions and convince people to talk to him about her and the circumstances of her death.

The minute he stepped out of the auto-drive cab, he wished he hadn't. The air stank. All around him people rushed about so quickly they almost pushed him off- balance several times. It seemed like the pedestrians were moving too quickly for his navigator to sense they were there, an undocumented "feature" of the device he'd have to investigate sometime.

"Hey, Buddy, don't you smell that? There's a sewage leak. The whole area is being evacuated. Get back in that cab before it drives away."

But, the warning came too late. The sound of the car's engine faded quickly. The tone from his navigator confirmed the cab was speeding away.

The noxious odor of sewage surrounded him, and he wished his sense of smell wasn't so keen. His dead eyes burned from the combined scents of rotten eggs, ammonia, and urine. There must be some way to get away, but how? All around him people scrambled to find shelter from the fumes. Even in the best of times few people ever paid attention to a blind man in need. Now, no one paid him any mind. Under normal circumstances he loathed being the focus of attention, or asking for help, but this was an emergency.

"I need help," he shouted. "I'm blind."

"Come with me," he heard a man say. A strong grip pulled at his arm. "This stuff really stinks. Let's get you out of here."

"Thank you. I guess this was a bad time to come downtown."

"Were you here for anything specific? You're right in front of the police station, you know. Is there something we could help you with?"

"You're a policeman, then? What luck! I came downtown to find out if you knew anything about my girlfriend's death."

"I'm Sergeant Michael Granger. I was just leaving the station when I heard you yell out. Let's get you someplace a bit safer and more comfortable. You don't look too well."

"Thank you, Sergeant. I think it's these fumes. I've got a nasty headache and I'm feeling rather dizzy."

"Hmm, headache and dizzy, huh? I'm taking you to the

hospital. My car is just around the corner. It'll be faster than calling an ambulance, especially at this time of day."

People always overreacted. Douglas knew it, but still hated when it happened. To most people, it seemed, his blindness equaled dependence. But, in truth, he was physically healthy and, in more ways than he could count, more independent than most people he knew.

"I don't think that's necessary, Sergeant. I'll be fine. I just need to get away from these fumes."

"My point exactly. At the hospital you'll be away from them, and we can get you checked out at the same time. No charge. It's all part of the service."

"I'm just a visitor to Chicago, but the police in New York City don't provide that kind of service."

"New York, huh? Well, I won't hold that against you as long as you don't hold the sewage leak against us."

"Listen, Sergeant, I appreciate your kindness. I really hate hospitals. Every time I'm in one it's a bad experience. I'm sure I'll be okay."

"Okay. I can't force you, but I really think you should be checked out. At the very least let me take you to your hotel. Where are you staying?"

Since the cab left him high and dry anyway, he saw no reason to reject the man's offer just to, stubbornly, assert his independence. He told Granger the name of his hotel.

"I know the place. I pass it often on my way home, and that's where I'm headed anyway."

Douglas heard the lie in the other man's voice, the gentle shift in pitch and timbre, but decided not to draw attention to it.

"It's too bad it's not the original building," Granger

continued. "It was unique."

"When I made the reservation I wasn't aware the original building had fallen victim to an earthquake. Still, it is a nice hotel, just not the architectural masterpiece I had planned to explore."

"Forgive me for asking this, but how does a blind man explore architecture?"

"No need to apologize. I'm asked that question often. It's simple really. You would use your eyes. I use my fingers. It's not quite the same thing, but I've gotten pretty good at getting an impression of what something looks like just by running my fingers over it. In fact, that's what I did yesterday at the Tribune building."

Granger sat quietly for a moment. "The Tribune building was an interesting place. I loved looking at it and I'm going to miss it, as I'm sure many people will."

"I heard on the radio this morning it had collapsed, apparently shortly after my visit. Such a shame."

"I'm glad you got away without injury. Hmm, I'm sorry. I've been rude. I neglected to ask your name."

Douglas introduced himself, holding out his hand and waiting for the other man to grasp it.

"Abledan? What an interesting name."

"It's Arabic, I think. Apparently one of my ancestors came from the Middle East. No one in my family ever talked about it much, unfortunately. I wish I knew more."

"Genealogy is an interest of mine. My own family is German, both sides. I've learned quite a bit, though of course the history gets a bit muddy around the time of the Second World War. Anyway, you said you were coming to the station to look into the death of someone?"

"My girlfriend. Actually, we just recently started seeing each other." This wasn't a lie, since they'd first met each other on the plane. "Her name was Dr. Cara Cordelia. A reporter on the radio said she died while participating in a conference. I want to know how and why she died. I need to know. She seemed healthy enough the last time I saw her a couple of days ago."

"I suppose I can do some checking for you, Mr. Abledan. But, you're not family, and I don't know how much information can be made available to you."

The car came to a gentle stop. Douglas opened the passenger door, feeling a rush of cool air hit his face, then turned back to face the driver.

"I'd appreciate anything you can find out, Sergeant. Thank you for the ride."

Now the die was cast. How they would land, Douglas could only guess.

* * *

Ed Grimes started working as a diener, or servant, at the county coroner two years ago. The twenty-five-year-old considered the morgue a stopping ground, a place to hang out and bide his time until he had a chance to do what he really wanted to do. He wasn't sure what his dream job would be, but he knew it wouldn't be in Chicago. The city had been a good place to grow up, but he wanted to see more of the world.

Grimes, a thin and gangly black man, never really fit in with others in his age group. Quieter, and more introspective, he enjoyed the peace and tranquility of the morgue. He could collect his thoughts here. The work he did suited him too. Helping to uncover the reasons for an individual's death made a difference, not only to the families, but to the authorities also.

Tying his smock behind his neck, he stretched two pair of rubber gloves over his hands, then walked to the bank of refrigerators. Examining the tags on each door, he pulled open the one containing the morgue's newest resident. Then, pulling out the slab, he eased her body onto a gurney, and rolled her over to one of the steel examination tables. Reverently, he eased her body onto the table, placed a rubber brick under her back to push her chest upward, laid her arms at her sides, and draped a sheet over the bottom half of her body. She was a beautiful woman, even in death. About fifty years old, with dark, curly hair sprinkled with grey.

Dr. David Hills, the chief coroner, was a burly man who kept his sixty-year-old body in tip-top condition. When he walked into the autopsy room a few minutes later, he looked calm, cool, and kempt. He wasn't the kind of man to let the pressure of his job become stressful. Too many people he knew died from coronary disease and he did not want to suffer the same fate. Several years ago, he began to study both yoga and tai chi in an effort to stave off the ill effects of his job. By all accounts the combined practices were working.

"What have we got today, Ed?"

"This woman was brought in last night. Apparently she collapsed and died, just as she was about to give some kind of lecture at the University."

"Such a shame."

Hills leaned over the body to read the tag on her toe.

"What killed you, Dr. Cordelia?"

"I don't think she can answer that for you, Doctor," Grimes said with a grin.

"No, I suppose not. But it never hurts to ask, does it? Let's get started, shall we? I trust the recorder is switched on?"

Grimes nodded.

"She was beautiful," he acknowledged, "in a plain sort of way, I mean. A bit on the heavy side though. Probably had a desk job. From the looks of her she wasn't too vain about her appearance. Her hair isn't dyed."

"Today is September twenty-first, two-thousand and twenty-one," Hills said into the air. "The time is fifteen-thirty hours. In attendance are Edward Grimes and Dr. David Hills. Autopsy of a Caucasian woman of roughly fifty years of age."

Taking a wand off a nearby table, Hills waved it from the top of the woman's head to the bottom of her feet.

"Five foot six inches tall," the device's metallic voice called out.

He pushed a button on the table. Another voice announced her weight, one hundred and fifty pounds, before displaying the information on a small screen by the body's hand.

"Examination of the lower extremities, notably of the right foot, finds evidence consistent with diabetic peripheral neuropathy. Ulcerations appear under the first and fifth metatarsal heads. The lesions are hyperkeratotic, with central tissue breakdown and necrosis beneath areas of increased plantar pressure. You had some trouble with your feet, didn't you, Doctor Cordelia?"

He took a moment to glance up at Grimes and wink. Some of the assistants questioned why he'd always address the deceased by name. Doing so, he'd respond, individualized each case and gave him a sense of empathy he believed necessitated a more thorough examination.

"The left wrist is pale. The faint outline of a wristwatch is visible. Several small, fatty deposits appear centralized on the posterior surface of the wrist."

With a small scalpel, he took a sample of the tissue, then moved on to look under the woman's hair, in her eyes and behind her ears.

"All right, I think we're ready to go inside now, Ed. Would you do the honors, please?"

Selecting a large scalpel from the table, Grimes pushed it deep into the body until he felt the tip hitting bone. Then he drew the blade through the flesh, cutting a Y-shaped incision, the arms of the Y extending from the front of each shoulder to the bottom end of the breastbone. Opening a woman's body called for a slightly different incision, the upper arms of the incision needed to curve around the breasts instead of cutting straight through them. The tail of the Y extended from the sternum down to the pubic bone.

After making the initial incision the younger man put down the large scalpel and, selecting a significantly smaller blade, began to peel back the skin, muscle, and soft tissues from the chest wall, laying the flap formed by the upper half of the Y over the dead woman's face. This was the part of an autopsy he had not gotten used to, and probably never would. The odor arising from the inside of a dead body was not unlike that of raw meat. To a vegetarian, like himself, there were few worse smells.

He put down the scalpel and, using an electric saw, cut along each side of the rib cage, allowing the chest plate to be lifted off and the body's internal organs to be exposed for Hills's examination. The job finished, Grimes stepped back away from the body.

"No, my boy, you're not quite done."

"Doctor?"

"Please, draw off some blood, urine, and bile for examination; we need to do a tox screen on her."

Grimes proceeded to fill three large syringes with samples of the requested fluids from various points in the body. Later, Hills would walk him through the toxicology tests he wanted performed.

When Grimes finished, Hills selected a small scalpel from the table and, with the finesse of a master painter, opened the pericardial sac around the heart. Then, with another quick, practiced stroke, he sliced open the pulmonary artery where it exited the heart. Gingerly he pushed his right index finger into the artery.

"Well," he said after a moment of probing. "There's no clotting which means she probably didn't die from an embolism. That would have been too easy anyway, wouldn't it? We need to look further."

Using the same scalpel, Hills proceeded to cut muscle tissue away from the bottom of the rib cage and diaphragm, until the flaps of abdominal wall fell to the side exposing the organs, which would later be removed for examination. One organ in particular, the heart, drew his attention. It appeared to be much larger than he'd normally expect in a fifty-year-old woman. He made a note to examine it more closely.

Blind Traveler's Blues

* * *

Orlando Hernandez walked through his cornfield with tears rolling down his cheek. Each day he walked through the field, just like his father and grandfather before him. Like them, he stayed vigilant, making sure his crop was well taken care of, and each stalk grew straight, tall, and green. Each of the previous season's crops produced an abundance of ears with yellow, plump kernels. Though this summer had been somewhat dry, enough rain fell to insure a large and successful yield. But, in his thirty-five years of life on the farm, he had never encountered a disease like the one currently ravaging the infant ears. The symptoms seemed similar to those of two groups of disease, smut, and rust, but this infection spread quicker than anything he'd seen before.

Hernandez surveyed the field, noting how many of the plants held droopy, black-spotted leaves. He knew, if he pulled the fine strands of husk off the ears of those plants, he would find white, pustuled galls instead of yellow, ripening kernels. And, though the corn stalks were growing, the rows no longer stood straight; meaning crosspollination probably would not take place. If it failed to occur, his crop could completely collapse. To make matters worse, no one knew the cause of the disease currently raging through the Valley of Mexico, or how to cure it.

The family had depended on their corn crop for the past three generations. Not only was it a source of food for the entire extended family, it also provided the income, allowing them to live in relative comfort. Now, with seven stomachs to fill, Hernandez didn't know how they would

104

survive.

Searching the field for his eldest son, he found the younger man crouched down next to a row of five-foot-tall plants, reaching low to pull one of the many diseased plants from the ground.

*He'll make a fine farmer one day, if we survive this disease.*

"Alberto, go find out what your mother is making for lunch. I'm starving."

When the young man vanished from sight, Hernandez knelt down on his knees and sobbed. He dreamt of leaving the farm to his children, just as his father and grandfather had done, but given the state of the crops now, the dream seemed more a fantasy. He looked up at the sky, clasped his hands together, and began to pray.

"Father, we don't talk as much as we should. I know this, but I hope you hear me now. We are desperate. Our lives are simple, but even the little we need seems to be taken away from us. Please, help us through this difficult time."

Hernandez crossed himself, then stood up slowly, hoping God heard the desperation in his voice. Without His intervention, there would be nothing left.

# CHAPTER SEVEN
*Day 6*


"There's a guy here to see you, Sarge. Wouldn't say what he wanted. Said you'd know. Name is Able-something, I think."

Granger shifted his gaze from the LCD screen in front of him. Joe Shapiro, a clerk from the Public Affairs office, loomed in the doorway, shifting his massive body from one foot to the other, waiting for a response.

"Seems like a strange kinda guy. Blind I think. Though, he keeps moving his head around, like he's looking around the place. It's kinda creepy."

"Thanks. I'll take it from here."

Despite Shapiro's warning, the man standing at the front desk surprised him.

"Is everything alright, Mr. Abledan?"

Douglas paused for a moment. "I came to see you because I was thinking about Cara's death"

"I'm not sure I follow."

"I wanted you to know I'm going back to Capone's this afternoon. I want to talk to the waitress that served Cara and me."

"I don't understand. What do you hope to learn from a waitress?

"I'm not sure, frankly, but I noticed something odd when she served our drinks, a funny aroma. I thought I recognized the smell, but couldn't place where I'd first smelled it, then I realized it was the same aroma that arose from the tea the attendant served to Cara on the plane from New York. I think there may be some kind of connection between the two women who served us."

"You got that just from a smell? That's a bit of a leap isn't it?"

"Maybe, but I'm going to look into it anyway. I have to. Look, Sergeant, I'm not here to ask your permission. I'm just here giving you notice of my whereabouts. It's something my Aunt Joan drummed into me."

Granger shook his head. "You've lost me. Why tell me?"

"Once, when I was eight years old, I went to stay overnight at my aunt and uncle's apartment in Queens."

"That's nice."

"Anyway, when I woke up the next morning, I decided to go to the corner store to get some candy. I didn't tell anyone I was going. When I got back, my aunt read me the riot act. She said people shouldn't go running off without saying where they were going, and she made me promise to always make sure someone knew where I was. So, I'm telling you where I will be, just in case something happens."

* * *

"Ernesto, I need to talk to you."

The woman's voice sounded even more shrill than usual.

"Are you alright, Lucy?"

"No. I'm not. Who was the woman in your apartment?"

107

"A neighbor," he lied. "She needed to get away from her husband so I offered her my couch for the night."

"Do all your neighbors walk around your apartment with no clothes on? Why was she wet and wrapped in *my* towel? Why would she tell me it was her apartment? Why were you naked?"

The more she ranted, the more her words muddled together, until she swallowed half of them.

"I wasn't naked."

"Ernesto, I saw you. It was dark in the room, but I saw you, and you had nothing on. Now, who was she? How long have you been sleeping with her behind my back?"

"Lucy, please calm yourself. You're misinterpreting the situation."

"Am I really?"

"Of course you are. Now please, why don't you come here for dinner tonight and I'll explain the whole thing to you. Wouldn't that be better than talking about this over the phone? You never know who might me listening in these days."

"Dinner?"

Tanner drew in a deep breath.

"At your place?" Her tone softened. "That does sound nice. You've never cooked for me before, Ernesto."

"Then it's about time I did, don't you think? Eight o'clock? I'll make your favorite, a mushroom casserole."

She sniffled. "Alright, but there's something else too. You know the friend you asked me to help you play the trick on?"

"What about her?"

"I just heard the news. She died."

"Yes, she did. It's very sad."

"I know she was a friend of yours. I'm so sorry, honey. Do you think she was allergic to the stuff you asked me to put in her drink? It's so horrible to think that could have happened."

"You have such a wild imagination, Lucy. I assure you it was only a juvenile prank. The chemical was harmless, something to make her feel the need to get to a bathroom, often. I would not injure her, nor ask you to participate in something that might have caused harm."

"Okay, honey. If you're sure. But just in case, maybe we should tell the police."

"No. Don't do that."

"Okay, honey. I just thought maybe they should know."

"Trust me, it would only complicate their investigation, and for no reason. Just come for dinner tonight and we'll talk about everything. Eight o'clock. I can't tell you how much I want to see you."

The phone went dead before Lucy could respond. She replaced it on its base, but wanted to pick it up again almost immediately. An unexpected thought entered her mind. The other day, when she'd brought breakfast to Ernesto's apartment, the woman who answered the door wore a perfume whose aroma smelled just like the liquid Ernesto asked her put into Cordelia's drink. Having been so incensed by the sight of another woman in her boyfriend's apartment, especially one without clothes on, it hadn't registered at the time. But now, replaying the scene in her mind, she knew something wasn't right.

* * *

Douglas's jacket provided little protection from the onslaught of raindrops currently falling from the sky. They felt like lead pellets pelting every inch of his body. Nor did the thin material offer much of a shield from the driving wind. He imagined the experience as being similar to taking a shower with his clothes on. And, while his Fedora kept his hair dry, each drop of moisture landing on it echoed in his ears.

Despite the downpour, he needed to get to Capone's to speak to the waitress. After Cordelia's death, and his interview with Tuttle, he felt sure she could provide him with a piece of the puzzle. Was it a coincidence Cordelia died the day after having dinner with him at Capone's? Was it coincidence Tuttle smelled the same as the Old Fashioned Cordelia drank? No. There was some sort of connection. He simply needed to find it.

When he arrived at the restaurant Douglas shook himself off, slapping his hat against his knee to rid it of excess water.

"May I help you, Sir?"

The man standing before him spoke with a Southern twang tinged with a bit of annoyance, which made sense since Douglas arrived between the lunch and dinner shifts, a time the staff probably took to relax a bit. Furthermore, Douglas more resembled a wet rag than a human being, which meant additional clean-up for the staff.

"Sorry for the puddle I'm sure I'm making. The other night I was having dinner with a friend..."

"Was there a problem, Sir? I could get the manager." The voice switched from annoyance to marked disdain.

"Oh no. Nothing of the sort. Everything was excellent. We were waited on by a lovely woman in a beaded dress. I believe her name was Lucy. I was hoping to speak with her for a few minutes."

"I'm sorry, Sir. It is against policy for staff members to fraternize with customers."

Douglas shook his head. "Perhaps I'm not making myself clear. The person with whom I had dinner here died the next day."

Douglas heard the other man suck in a quick breath.

"I'm terribly sorry, Sir. I'm sure it was not due to anything she'd eaten here. We've never had a case of food poisoning. Never even a single health code violation. Please, let me get the manager."

"Forgive me for not being clear, again, I'm not here to assign blame. I'm simply trying to cover all bases, because I need to understand why Cara died. That's why I want to speak to Lucy. If anything, it was Cara's fault for having a drink. I know now I should have stopped her. She suffered from diabetes. But you know how women can be, and one drink didn't seem like much of anything."

"I understand, Sir. My wife can be insistent too. If you'll give me a few minutes to check, I think Lucy is on today."

Douglas listened to muffled footfalls fading into the distance. While he waited for their return, the sounds of the room came into sharper focus. To his left a fish tank's filter gurgled. Down the hall a guitar and a saxophone tried to harmonize. Above his head the buzz of florescent lights sounded like a swarm of angry bees. He'd always hated the noise florescent bulbs made, and marveled no one else seemed to be bothered by it. Now the sound mingled in his head with the fish tank filter and the two off-key instruments to create a conflagration of noise he found hard to ignore. Suddenly, his ears picked up a new sound, a woman's footsteps coming toward him.

"I'm Lucy Tanner." The woman's voice sounded as thin and shrill as Douglas remembered it. She spoke quickly, a sign she might be unsure of herself. "I was told you wanted to talk to me."

"I don't know if you remember me."

"Sure I do. We don't get many blind customers. You were in on Saturday night."

*Excellent memory.* "The reason for my visit today pertains to the woman who accompanied me that night. You may have just been informed she died the next day."

Tanner sucked in a mouthful of air, a sound not unlike a vacuum cleaner pulling in its first breath after being activated.

"I didn't have to be told. I heard about it on TV this morning. It's just awful. How did she die?"

"That's why I'm here. All I know is she wasn't feeling well when we left here, and the next day she was dead."

Tanner fell silent for a few moments, but the floor squeaked under her feet.

"Um. I don't know what to say, Mr...."

"Abledan. Douglas Abledan. Thank you. As I was telling the gentleman, Cara's death might have been her own fault. She was a diabetic and probably shouldn't have had the drink you brought her."

Suddenly the aroma of perspiration hit Douglas's nostrils. It hadn't been there a moment ago. Something he'd said alarmed the woman, something other than the news of Cordelia's death. The woman's voice, shakier and higher pitched the longer she spoke, along with her sweating, made him wonder what he was missing.

"Um. Was there a problem with the drink? You could have told me. I would have gladly brought another."

Douglas shook his head. "No. The drink and the food were both quite delicious, but the drinks we ordered were quite sweet and possibly pushed her blood sugar over some kind of edge."

The aroma of sweat became stronger, and the creaking of the floorboards sped up, with each passing moment.

"Oh my God!" The woman's voice rose to a shrill. "Could one drink really have done that?"

"Please, I didn't mean to imply anything or implicate you in any way. I'm not saying the drink you brought her caused her death. I'm just looking into all possibilities. Thank you for your time. I should let you get back to work now."

Douglas seemed to have hit another roadblock, or had he?

*She's hiding something, and it's making her nervous.*

* * *

When Carl Bruckner, Capone's night manager, heard a woman sobbing in the foyer of the restaurant, he put down his pen and hurried from the reservation desk toward the sound.

A man in a blue jacket and black Fedora hat pushed his way past the restaurant's heavy door. Lucy Tanner had her face buried in her hands.

"Lucy, are you alright? Did that man hurt you?"

"N-no," the waitress said, wiping a tear from her eye. "He was in here a few days ago. He just told me the woman he'd had dinner with died the next day."

"And he blamed you?"

Her head quickly bobbed back and forth twice. A tear ran down her cheek. "No."

She gulped back another tear, and focused on the man speaking to her. He was her boss, and they didn't always get along well, but now he showed her a kind face and sympathetic eyes.

"He was just looking for answers, a possible cause of her death. He actually blamed the woman herself for having the drink I served them. He thought it could have been bad for her, because she was diabetic."

"I see. I've known a few people who had diabetes. None of them ever touched a drop. Diabetics shouldn't drink alcohol. But one drink shouldn't have killed her."

"That's what I told him, but I don't know if he believed me.

"Why wouldn't he? You told him the truth."

Lucy pulled a tissue from her pocket and dabbed the corner of her eyes. "I don't know, but people don't always believe the truth."

Bruckner frowned. "I'll talk to him if he comes back, Lucy. You best get along back to work now. The dinner crowd will be filtering in soon."

"Thank you, Mr. Bruckner." She flashed him a shy grin, trying to create the pretense of calm.

After the woman walked back toward the dining room,

Bruckner glanced at the door. Something told him this wouldn't be the last time he'd cross paths with the man in the Fedora.

* * *

Lucy Tanner stood in front of the door to Ortega's apartment, fishing in her purse for her compact. Finally flipping the compact open, she checked her makeup, smoothing down an errant eyebrow hair. Then, running her hands down her body, she tugged at the hem of her tight-fitting, red dress. Ortega hated wrinkled clothing, and bumps and lines under clothing too, so she had left her bra in her locker at Capone's. Her breasts ached without the support, a small price to pay if it meant keeping her boyfriend happy, and she wanted tonight to be perfect.

A moment later, the door opened and Ortega stood before her with a glass of white wine in his hand. As always, he dressed immaculately, in a dark blue suit, yellow necktie, and blue-and-yellow-striped shirt. Music, from inside the apartment, caressed her ears while Ortega's eyes slowly explored her body, sending a shiver down her spine.

"You look good enough to eat, Lucy, dear," he said, stepping aside to let her pass. "But we'll save that for dessert." He twisted the end of his mustache between two fingers and winked.

"Thank you, honey."

Ortega helped her slide out of her overcoat, detaching its satin lining when it snagged on the metallic fabric of her dress. Then, after handing her a glass of wine, he led her into a richly appointed room lit by candles casting soft, shimmering shadows upon the walls.

Taking a sip from her glass, and looking out at the lake through the apartment's bay window, Tanner realized she should have been happy. She wanted to be here, with the man she loved, but the blind man's visit earlier in the day weighed heavily on her mind. She couldn't help wondering if, inadvertently, she'd had something to do with his companion's death.

"Dinner will be ready in a few minutes," Ortega called from the kitchen. "I made a special mushroom casserole. My own recipe. I hope you like it."

Absently, Tanner sniffed the air. "I'm sure it will be delicious."

* * *

Douglas put his judo uniform into the gym bag he brought with him from home, then sat on the bed to meditate, attempting to put himself into a relaxed state of mind and body before working out, a practice he'd begun when he first started taking classes in the martial arts. But, a clear mind wasn't easy to achieve today. One by one he focused on each event as it occurred during his short time in Chicago. The Chicago Tribune building fell. Cara Cordelia died. He wasn't sure how much more sadness his mind could hold.

Finally, the images faded and, for the next twenty minutes, he sat motionless, breathing rhythmically. When he finally opened his eyes and began moving, his movements were slow and measured. His hand trailed down to his wrist, probing the face of his watch rather than pushing the voice-activator. It was later than he'd thought. Still, it was such a nice night, he decided to forgo the taxi and walk to the dojo.

The forty-five minute walk down Michigan Avenue, he decided, would limber him up, and give him time to wrestle with his expectations for the workout. He'd discovered long ago, expectations seldom served him well. They often led to worry. Working out at this dojo did worry him though. It would be a new experience, and since his accident he hadn't always been fond of new experiences. People sometimes acted strangely when dealing with a blind man. Though others soon followed, he'd been the first blind student to enroll at the dojo in New York. It took the sighted students a full six months before they realized they could work him hard.

As he walked, Douglas listened to the buildings calling to him. His navigator could tell him the names of buildings if they were incorporated into the electronic maps stored in the computer he wore. But, even those without a name seemed to have their own personality. Back in New York, the building he worked in had a deep, decidedly male quality to it. Now, as he walked past the site of the Tribune, he remembered its "voice," old and authoritative, just as a building with its reputation should have sounded. A chill ran down his spine.

Douglas felt tired, but pleased with his decision to walk from the hotel. Now limber and warm, he could handle whatever the judo instructor threw at him. Turning his attention back to the navigator he knew his destination neared. By the smell of stale beer and marijuana, and the broken English of the few conversations he heard, he could tell, he wasn't in the best neighborhood. In a few minutes he stood in front of the Blue Dragon Judo Academy.

Opening the door, he was immediately put at ease by the scent of jasmine, one of his favorite incense aromas and the same scent wafting through the dojo back in New York. He turned off his navigator and reached for the sonic cane in his pocket.

When a feminine voice greeted him, Douglas introduced himself, explaining he'd called yesterday to inquire about taking a class while in town.

"Please come in, Mr. Abledan. We were about to begin."

The woman's footfalls moved away, but returned quickly, accompanied by those of a man whose pungent aroma permeated the air. His breathing was quick and shallow.

"Sensei Thomans," the woman began, "this is Douglas Abledan. He would like to join us in class today."

Douglas bowed toward the sound.

"Mr. Abledan? We spoke on the phone, didn't we?"

"Yes, Sir. We did. I'm glad you remember."

"You said you had attained the rank of *Yonkyu?* If so, you know all the basic moves we'll be doing tonight. Did you bring a uniform? I don't allow anyone inside the dojo unless they are properly dressed, a sign of respect I'm sure you understand."

"I have my gear right here."

Douglas patted the blue, suede bag at his side.

"Use the restroom to change. We'll get started after you're ready. Excuse me while I find someone to work with you."

After a few minutes Thomans returned, accompanied by a man who walked with a distinct limp.

"Mr. Abledan, I'd like to introduce Eduardo Ortega. He has graciously agreed to be your partner."

"Mr. Abledan..." the new man began.

"Please call me Douglas, since we are about to work together."

"You may call me Eduardo. I'd be honored to work with you. I've worked with several blind students before and have both enjoyed the experience and learned a great deal from them."

For the next hour, Douglas sweated and strained his body. He fought off attack after attack while he and Ortega went through their drills. After thirty minutes, Thomans ordered the students to take turns sparring with each other. When his turn arrived, Thomans clapped his hands once to signal he and Ortega should move forward until they made contact.

During their match, Douglas deflected every attempt Ortega made to unbalance him and knock him to the mat. They finished when Douglas rolled onto his back, flipping his opponent over his body, and then quickly moving to pin him. By the time the class ended, he had learned several new moves, and had flipped and pinned most of the other students.

Changing back into his street clothes, Douglas mulled over the experiences of the past hour. Something just didn't feel right. The dojo smelled right. He had no complaints about the caliber of the work out. Something odd about the people, perhaps? They exuded a kind of energy unfamiliar to him. It wasn't necessarily bad energy, but it didn't make him overly comfortable either.

*Ah well, I'll be returning to New York, and my own*

*dojo, soon anyway.*

"Douglas," Ortega called, "would you join me for some coffee? I'd like to hear your impressions of our class."

"Why not? I could use the time to wind down. That was an intense class."

"They always are."

Walking down the street with Ortega, one particular building, the James Charnley House, caught Douglas's attention. Built in 1892 in collaboration with Frank Lloyd Wright, it was considered, by some, to be the architecture world's first modern house. He stopped for a moment, tempted to explore it right then, but decided doing so would have been rude.

"You've got talent, Douglas. Where did you learn to move like that?"

"I started taking judo while still in rehab, after my accident. A little over two years ago. Since then, I've found a great teacher."

"It shows. I had a hard time keeping up in there."

"You did pretty well," Douglas said, patting his side gingerly. "I've got the bruises to prove it."

"I didn't hurt you, did I? I was trying to go easy on you since this was our first time together."

Douglas chuckled. "Nothing permanent. One always remembers his first time, and the bruises will help remind me."

After about ten minutes, Ortega led Douglas into a smoke-filled coffee shop reminiscent of Sid's office back in New York. They skirted tables and people, relying more on Ortega's knowledge of the place than the pulses from Douglas's cane, until finally finding an empty table.

"This isn't a fancy place," Ortega began once they were seated, "but I've found it to be a good place to unwind after working out. Their coffee has a hint of chicory. It's exquisite. So, tell me, what brought you to Chicago?"

"Strictly vacation, until my boss told me to meet with a new client, 'as long as I'm going to be there anyway, he said.' And you? What do you do when you're not beating people up at the dojo?"

"I'm the director of the Agricultural Pathology department at the University of Illinois."

*What an unexpected, and interesting, coincidence.*

Douglas's elation quickly faded when he asked about Cordelia, and Ortega paused for what felt like an inordinately long time before answering.

"I met Dr. Cordelia," Ortega said stiffly, "but only recently, at the conference we're hosting now. I knew her by reputation, of course. A very smart woman, an expert in her field, which is why she was invited. You have my sincere condolences."

Ortega's sympathetic words rang hollow in Douglas's ears. He seemed genuinely disinterested in Cordelia's death, which didn't make sense considering they were colleagues. The man's intonation sounded almost mechanical. Something disturbed him about the man's demeanor too, but he couldn't quite put his finger on it. He didn't pick up any of the usual signals suggesting the man was lying. But, in such a noisy room, filled with the aromas of food, he had a difficult time hearing Ortega's inflections, or detecting his bodily secretions. At the very least he wasn't telling everything he knew. When the waitress came to take their orders, he seemed to be relieved by the interruption.

"Ruby, this is my friend, Douglas Abledan. He's here all the way from New York. Came to work out at my dojo."

"All the way from New York? Don't they have martial arts schools in New York?"

"Yes, of course, dear lady. As I was just explaining, I'm on vacation, and I decided to visit the dojo while in town."

"Well, Ortega here is a good man. I'm sure he'll take care of you."

"Oh, yes, he is."

The waitress walked slowly away from the table. Before turning his attention back to Ortega, Douglas listened to a couple of the other customers teasing her.

*So crude.* "Is the University doing any research about that new corn disease I've heard about?"

"Yes. That's the subject of our conference. In fact, Dr. Cordelia was trying to identify the pathogen for us so we could devise a cure."

There, he'd heard it again; the hint of inflection suggesting Ortega could be trying to hide something. His curiosity piqued, but no matter how many questions he asked, he learned little more about Cordelia's tragic demise. Ortega told him she had been part of a team of scientists. But, he said, for security purposes, the substance of the conference and any related research remained confidential. Clearly, he had no intention of pursuing the matter further.

* * *

While scanning stations on his car's radio, Ortega caught the beginning of a news program. The announcer described a report recently issued by The Mexican

Department of Health painting a very grim picture of the wide-scale effects of the disease decimating the nation's corn crop.

"As we reported yesterday, according to agricultural experts, this year's corn crop yield is projected to be only one quarter of last year's. This, in turn, they say, has reduced the availability of the corn meal used to make one of the country's food staples, tortillas. Subsequently, the cost of tortillas has been rising at an accelerated rate. With half of Mexico's population living on no more than the equivalent of five dollars a day, an alarming number of people are dying of starvation. Mexico's President, Emanuel Hasta, has tried to put a cap on the price of tortillas, to no avail. Retailers insist they have to meet the rising cost of corn meal, and still make a profit. Negotiations are continuing."

The announcer paused to take a deep breath before continuing his report.

"In a related story, the U.S. Department of Agriculture today released a report saying the disease infecting Mexican corn crops has spread across the border. Farmers in American border states are pleading with the government for help, but so far, aside from setting up an investigatory conference, nothing has been done."

Smiling, Ortega leaned forward and switched off the radio.

*It seems Gaia will exact her punishment with the help of those she is punishing.*

For twenty minutes, the Escalade negotiated the city's streets, in slowly falling rain, before arriving at a large, squat, red-brick building, the current meeting place for the Chicago cell of Gaia's Children. The group changed locations weekly to avoid being infiltrated by any of the dozen law enforcement agencies who considered it an enviro-terrorist organization, a charge Ortega considered ridiculous. Granted, they committed some serious acts, like the bombing of the Unimat building in New York a few weeks ago, but sometimes violence became a necessity in defense of important ideas. And, what could be more important than defending the Earth against those who would do her harm? Gaia would have destroyed the building herself, in self-defense, if she had been able to. The Children were just helping her.

Cells of Gaia's Children criss-crossed the planet, each charged with a different mission. The men and women comprising Ortega's cell prevented interference from those who could mitigate the results of natural disasters. The corn plague exemplified that goal. It began quite naturally, with the release of dormant spores. The group intended to make sure the ensuing disease ran its course. Gaia, after all, unleashed the spores to punish humanity for its sins

# CHAPTER EIGHT
*Day 7*

Dr. Hills was just finishing his autopsy report on Cordelia when Detective Harris walked into his office. The woman died a very painful and protracted death. No doubt an insidious murderer roamed the city.

"Okay, Dr. Hills," Harris said, pulling a voice recorder from his pocket and switching it on. "What do you have for me? Do you have a cause of death yet?"

"Unfortunately."

"Unfortunately? Your job is to find causes of death. When you do so shouldn't you be happy about it?"

Hills shook his head.

"I suppose you're right. I just wish this poor woman hadn't died in such prolonged agony."

"I assume you mean she'd didn't die from a sudden heart attack, as was originally suggested."

"Oh, no. This poor woman was poisoned."

"Poisoned? Are you sure?"

"Furthermore, the poison had to be introduced over a period of time, during which she would have suffered a great deal. She was diabetic, which would have confused her understanding of the symptoms she was experiencing. Many of them, you see, commonly accompany her type of diabetes. She wouldn't necessarily have known she was dying. At most she would have thought she had some kind of flu.

"The particular poison she ingested, Pulegone, comes from an herb called Pennyroyal, a plant native to Kentucky, often used in the past as a means of inducing abortion in pregnant women. It's extremely toxic. It wouldn't have taken much to kill her."

Harris had been a cop for many years. In all that time, he wondered, how hadn't he heard of this particular poison.

"The herb has a sweet taste and aroma," Hills continued. "If the poison had been mixed with something that is normally very sweet, she wouldn't necessarily have noticed any difference in taste or smell. I suppose that's something for you to check into.

"As for me, my job is done here. The woman had an enlarged heart, and many of her internal organs were in the process of shutting down. Those symptoms, in some cases, could be the result of prolonged diabetes, but not here. She probably collapsed initially from severe insulin shock. The poison would have thrown her blood sugar, which was already compromised by diabetes, completely out of whack. Her blood sugar level was through the roof. She probably went into convulsions and died."

Harris stopped the recording, then searched the device's menu for the notes he'd taken at the university. Finding the report, he pulled the speaker next to his ear and listened to his own voice for a few minutes before returning his gaze toward the coroner.

"That was what the witnesses reported."

"The BS levels alone would have killed her if left untreated," Hills added. "But it definitely was the poison that did the job. The level of toxin I found in her blood and organs indicate she had been ingesting it for quite some time, at least a month. Her murderer had to be somebody who knew about poisons, how quickly they act in the body and how easily detectible they are. Many are very detectible, as is this one, but only if you're specifically looking for it. I would assume she went to the doctor regularly, to check up on her diabetes and to find out about these symptoms as they developed. But unless the doctor was looking for something specific he might not do the right tests and might dismiss the whole thing as a case of the flu, as I said previously. Some doctors aren't very thorough and they give a patient the easiest and most likely answers to symptoms. It's incompetence, if you ask me, but it happens often."

"One more thing, Doctor. This Pennyroyal plant you mentioned, is it indigenous to this area? I mean would the plant be easy enough to find so a sufficient quantity of the toxin could be extracted?"

"I just said so." Hills grumbled. "It is a common plant, found most often in Kentucky and the southern United States. In fact, at one time, it grew so plentifully an entire region of Kentucky was named after it. But it can be found in other places as well."

*Just great! The suspects are going to be piling up.*

# CHAPTER NINE

Garcia felt like a hostage. His frustration level rose while the switchboard operator at the University of Chicago, supposedly, sought someone for him to speak with. Finally, after ten minutes, he was reprieved.

"My name is Luiz Garcia. I'm with the University of Mexico. I received a message from a Dr. Cara Cordelia a few weeks ago, while I was on a dig site. She said she was headed to Chicago and that I should try to reach her there."

"I'm the director of this facility, Dr. Ernesto Ortega. Dr. Cordelia was one of the attendees at a conference we've been holding here."

"Was an attendee? Do you mean she is no longer there?"

"I'm sorry to be the one to have to tell you this, but Dr. Cordelia has passed away. Were you a friend of hers?"

"Well, um, no, but the message I received suggested my work might benefit one of her current projects. Frankly, I don't see how. She was an agricultural pathologist whereas I study the fossils left by plants to learn the history of vegetation."

Garcia had hoped he wouldn't have to explain himself, and, because the two fields were related, albeit distantly, he could incur some respect. But, that didn't seem likely.

"As I said, she was here," Ortega continued. "We've been researching ways to identify and combat a corn disease that's been rapidly spreading. I'm sure you've heard of it, since it seems to have begun in your country."

"Of course. Now I understand why she contacted me. I think the disease you've been researching might have begun at the dig site I was just working on. There was an accident involving an artifact."

"That's very interesting."

"Perhaps Dr. Cordelia thought I might have something to contribute to her research. She may have thought I'd make myself available to her. I don't usually do so, unless I see some benefit to my work."

"I understand. I'm not sure what her thinking was. I wasn't even aware she had contacted any outside resources and, I must say, I disagree with her assessment of our needs. I doubt an extra person, especially someone who is not an experienced pathologist, would be of much help. Now, if you will excuse me, I have other matters to attend to."

Garcia slammed the phone down. If Ortega wanted so much control of the research project, at the expense of a more thorough investigation, then so be it. In his mind, he fulfilled his obligation to the world.

* * *

"Elizabeth, we may have a problem."

Ortega watched the woman sitting opposite him brush a stray lock of hair away from her eyes. He knew her well enough to understand the movement signaled stress.

"Problem? What is it, 'nesto honey?"

Ortega glared at her. "I've asked you not to call me that, especially not at work. As I was saying, that call was from Mexico, from a man named Luiz Garcia. He wanted to talk to Dr. Cordelia."

"Who is he?" she asked, her eyes widening.

"An archeobotanist at the University of Mexico. Apparently, your friend Cara contacted him about the research we are doing here."

"Did he say what she had told him?"

Ortega shook his head. "Fortunately, she only left him a message. He was on some dig site at the time she called and didn't speak to him directly."

"Then I don't understand what the problem is."

"I tried to convince him we didn't need his help; that Cara had erred in contacting him. But, I'm not sure it's the last we've heard from him."

A sharp rap on the door interrupted the conversation. After a moment, the door opened and Detective Harris stuck his head into the room.

"Detective, please come in. That will be all for now, Dr. Tuttle."

As the woman walked out of the room, a minty aroma trailed behind her like an amorphous plume.

"This isn't a social call, Doctor," Harris said, once the two men were alone. "There's been a new development in the Cordelia case. In light of what I've recently learned from the coroner, this is now a murder investigation. I'll need to ask you and your staff a few more questions."

"Murder? How could that be? I assume this means you know what caused her death?"

"Yes, and this is particularly interesting considering the line of work you are all in. She was poisoned, using a plant extract."

"Well, yes, plants are what we deal with here,

Detective. Still, I can't imagine someone here poisoning her. What would be the motive?"

"I'm still looking into that. Tell me, have you heard of a plant called Pennyroyal?"

"It's a rather common plant. We don't deal with that kind of plant here though. We only deal with agricultural produce, food crops."

"So you said before, but that doesn't mean someone couldn't get their hands on it if they wanted to, does it? Can you think of anyone who might have a grudge against Dr. Cordelia? Professional jealousy, perhaps? You did say she was a leader in her field, didn't you? And, she was the head of a group searching for the identity of the virus currently infecting the corn plants? It seems to me that kind of thing would make her rather famous, and perhaps even rich."

"Yes," Ortega admitted pensively, "but I doubt anyone here would stoop to murder. All the scientists here are already world-renowned."

"Do any of us really feel we get enough recognition? People seek prestige for a wide range of reasons, Doctor, and use many methods, including murder, to acquire it. My job is to find out who commits those murders and what the particular reason is."

"I trust you're not accusing me, Detective? As I told you when we first met, I barely knew Dr. Cordelia, and I was attracted to her. Correct me if I'm mistaken but people don't usually murder those they are attracted to, do they?"

Harris shook his head. "I'm not accusing anyone, yet. I've just begun this investigation and don't have any leads. But, to answer your question, I have seen my share of crimes of passion."

"I see. Well, I'll have to inform the staff and visitors, of course."

"I'd prefer you didn't do that, not yet anyway. It's better if whoever did this thinks they got away with it. One last question, Doctor. I know many of the scientists attending your conference are from out of town. Could you tell me where Dr. Cordelia came from?"

"She lived in Ithaca, New York. She was on staff at Cornell University."

"I see. Well, thank you for your time."

Harris whispered a final note about the interview into his recorder.

* * *

To Sergeant Michael Granger, the Bureau of Investigative Services was a hallowed hall, the place he'd dreamed of working at ever since attending high school at Chicago's famed School of Leadership. Police work was in his blood. His father and grandfather both walked beats on the streets of this city. He'd been nurtured on stories of their exploits. Both were killed on the job. With any luck, his own life, and shoe leather, would be spared the same fate. He dreamt of reaching a goal neither of his forebears lived long enough to achieve, becoming a detective. But, after being on the force for ten years, he felt like his goal lay always just beyond his reach.

In order to help the blind man he'd met on the day of the sewage leak, Granger needed information only a detective could provide. But, because he was not on the team initiating the investigation into Cordelia's death, he fell out of the loop. There were rules and procedures for outsiders to acquire the kind of information he needed, but all of them took time. Abledan was only going to be in the city for a few days, not enough time for proper procedure. Still, he felt he needed to help Abledan in whatever way he could, though he couldn't exactly explain why. It wasn't a paternalistic reaction to someone he thought might be less capable than himself. He hated when people reacted to disability in such a manner. No, this felt more like something his wife, Tosha, might have called a spiritual connection with the man. By helping Abledan, in some way, he felt like he helped himself.

Granger wasn't the most politically correct person in the world, a point of constant concern for his wife. He had no problem with the thought of bypassing the chain of command in order to get what he needed. For the most part, people on the force appreciated his diligence and dedication and allowed him to bend the rules so long as no serious harm came from it. But, the man he needed to speak with, Detective Paul Harris, was a stickler for rules.

Granger met Harris five years earlier, during the investigation of a rather grisly drug-related murder the beat cop had literally stumbled upon. Harris disliked beat cops in general. He felt the strength of this, or any, police force lay in its detectives, not the cops patrolling the street. But, his almost immediate dislike of Granger went beyond his overall prejudice, primarily because he felt the younger man used his family's history with the force in order to get assigned to a relatively quiet precinct in the city. This was not true, but it was enough to create a barrier between the two men, one Granger believed to be insurmountable. When he'd arrived at Harris's desk he took a deep, calming breath before speaking.

"Detective, do you have a moment? I need some information."

Harris looked up from the paper he was studying. He rubbed his eyes and focused them on the man who had disturbed his concentration. His gaze moved slowly up Granger's body. It only took him a moment to recognize the man.

"What information would that be, Patrolman Granger, isn't it?"

Harris insisted on calling him a patrolman. It was, Granger suspected, an attempt at rattling his cage.

"Sergeant Michael Granger, Detective. I see you have as good a memory as ever. I was hoping to get a bit of information about a case you're working on."

"I don't forget rookies who mess up murder investigations, Granger," Harris sneered. "What case are you talking about? Why should I give you anything? Think you can mess this one up too?"

"I hoped we could move beyond the past; forget about old grudges and mistakes."

"You did, huh?"

Granger had never been one to hold grudges, unlike some people. Harris unfortunately was, so he decided it best to just get to the point of the encounter. He'd long ago given up trying to close the chasm between them.

"I heard you are the lead investigator on the Cordelia case, and was among the group of first responders."

"You heard right. So what? What do you know about the case? Who sent you?"

"I wasn't exactly sent to you. A man claiming to be Dr. Cordelia's boyfriend approached me. He wants to know what happened to her, of course."

"And he doesn't know to go through official channels, I suppose?"

"He was trying to do just that when we met on the day of the sewage leak. He had just arrived by taxi at the stationhouse. I gave him a lift back to his hotel and we talked."

"Nice of you. So what?"

"So, I told him I'd find out what I could. That's why I came to see you. Believe me you wouldn't have been my first choice. The point is, both he and Dr. Cordelia were visitors to Chicago, and I thought I should help as much as I could. So, I'll ask you again, what have you found out?"

"Look Granger, I know there are some people who let you get away with things around here, but I'm not one of them. You have to go through channels. There are departmental policies about how information is shared."

Granger's shoulders slackened. Rookies, fresh out of the academy often received this kind of dressing down, the "party" line. Harris, he'd heard, relished in repeating it. Now, all he could do was stand there and take it.

"I realize that. But, Mr. Abledan is not a resident of Chicago, as I've said. The process you suggest takes time to go through, something he doesn't have. Come on, Harris, give an inch for a change. It won't kill you and it would mean a lot to the woman's boyfriend."

"You've been on the force for this long and you still don't get it, do you?"

"Get what?"

"Procedure. Rules. Honor. You don't get any of it."

"Not when bending those rules helps protect someone, no, I don't."

"Well, you can't protect anyone here. The woman is already dead."

"But I can save this man from feeling trapped in some kind of emotional limbo."

"I'm afraid you can't even do that. Not if you tell him how she died. Not if you tell him she was murdered. You see, Granger, someone poisoned her. She ingested an extract from a plant called Pennyroyal. And that's all you're getting from me. Now, go away. Go study the manual. Learn proper procedure for these cases. One last thing for you to consider, Patrolman. You said the man who approached you wanting this information told you he was the woman's boyfriend, didn't you?"

"That's right. What of it?"

"Did it ever occur to you he could also be her murderer? Boyfriends often are, you know."

"No, I'll admit that never occurred to me. Did I neglect to mention the man is blind? How could a blind man commit such a murder?"

"It's been known to happen, Granger. Sick, depraved people find ways."

"But you just told me she was poisoned. How would a blind man orchestrate and carry out such a scheme? How would a blind man distill the poison? What would have been the motive?"

"The motive will take some investigation. As far as means goes, as I said, people find a way."

"It would seem to me, Detective, poisoning someone

takes a certain degree of expertise. The perpetrator has to know the poison and how it reacts on a victim. Abledan doesn't strike me as someone who has special knowledge in that area. He told me he was here on some sort of business enterprise."

"Ever hear of the Internet, Granger? Now there's a business enterprise for you. All sorts of information on there. And, I understand it's handicapped accessible. Besides, I shouldn't have to tell a police officer looks can be deceiving. When I first saw you I thought you were a real cop. Now I know better."

Granger ignored the insult. Responding to it wouldn't help him get answers. Scowling, he turned and began to walk out of the room.

"Now you've opened the door, so to speak, we can't let it close too quickly," Harris snapped. "Do you know which hotel Abledan is staying at?"

"The Crowne Plaza. Why?"

"Police work, Granger. You do remember how it's done, don't you? A woman is dead. I'm not as eager as you are to dismiss a boyfriend who might have reasons to murder her. I'll be sure to send your regards when I speak to him, though." Harris winked.

Granger rushed out of the room, before Harris had a chance to say something to earn him a punch in the mouth.

*Wonderful! Now Abledan is a suspect.*

* * *

Elizabeth Tuttle made her way to the lab assigned to Cordelia's group, but the journey tortured her. The two women had become friends, of a sort. Over the past few months, the two of them exchanged e-mails and phone calls, mostly about work, but some girl talk filtered in too. Invading Cordelia's space now felt like a betrayal.

Was she about to betray the rest of the world too? Ortega kept saying other people were the traitors, with their inconsiderate indifference to the Earth Mother, Gaia, and her needs. He said the corn plague punished humanity for their crimes. But, Tuttle wasn't so sure. If Ortega was correct would Gaia allow the scientists to continue trying to cure the disease?

In the end, her relationship with Ortega left little room for choice. Betraying him was not an option. Even if she had not pledged her heart to him, his temper scared her. She had not often witnessed it personally, but she saw the reminders of it, the scrapes and dents in his cane. It seemed like every few days another one appeared.

Most of the lights in the building were now shut off. Those still on illuminated rooms where the janitorial staff labored into the night. Tuttle clung to the shadows, glad she'd decided to wear dark clothing today. Of course, there were motion sensors set in strategic spots, to guard against industrial spies, but Ortega made sure she knew where they were secreted.

By the time she arrived at the lab, her nerves were frazzled. She almost pushed her card key into the slot next to the door, a mistake Ortega would have flown into a rage over. She reached into her pocket and pulled out the master key he had given her, a card used by the janitorial staff. Unlike most of the other keys, this one bore no name. She avoided another mistake by quickly recoiling from the light switch. The full moon cast a soft glow into the room. She waited until her eyes adjusted to the dim light, then, switching on the penlight Ortega instructed her to bring, walked to Cordelia's workstation.

Brushing a long strand of copper hair away from her eyes, she began rummaging over the tabletop. Immediately, a yellow envelope, half buried under a stack of printout paper to the left of the computer, caught her attention. The label read "Research Material: Corn Disease." This was what she needed, dated notes.

At first glance, the notes appeared to begin only shortly before the conference. However, on closer examination, she learned Cordelia thought quite a bit about the origin of the corn disease long before coming to Chicago. Both the older notes and the more recent ones were important. They showed a timeline of the progress Cordelia continued to make in her research on the origin of the disease. The disease demonstrated characteristics of two different types of pathogen. Tuttle already knew this. But, she discovered, Cordelia made a breakthrough. She'd isolated genetic markers. These, she believed, would allow her to trace the two viruses back to the common ancestor she believed was the source of the disease.

*They might find the cure with these notes. Let's see how I can "correct" Cara's work.*

While Tuttle's right hand busily forged new notes, her left hand fondled the three stones she always kept in her pocket. She was ten years old when she'd found them, on a beach during her family's last vacation together. She remembered the trip vividly. The stones, rubbed shiny and smooth from many years of handling, reminded her of a calmer time in her life, relaxing her whenever she felt stressed.

Finally, satisfied with her forgeries, she collected the original sheets of paper. Two words scribbled on the last page caught her attention, "Contact Garcia." So, this was the link to the mystery man, but why had Cordelia called him?

Putting the envelope back exactly where she found it, she collected a few things from her own workstation, then walked out of the lab, satisfied no one would be the wiser.

* * *

Sitting at a small table inside the coffee shop, Douglas contemplated the phone call he'd received from Granger. The man spoke hesitantly, saying he'd acquired some information, but refusing to give it to him over the phone. All the policeman would divulge was that the news would not please him. Granger seemed like a nice guy, but Douglas couldn't get past the feeling, because he had met him in a crisis situation, every encounter would be hazardous. Cops, no matter their good intentions, were always involved in crises.

"Could you please bring me a piece of the wonderful pie I ate the other night?" he regarded the waitress when she came to his table.

"Sure, Mr. Abledan. You waiting for Ortega again? He's always late, you know."

"Actually, no, I'm waiting for someone else. Please forgive me for saying so, dear lady, but I'm not in a very talkative mood right now. A good friend died recently."

"Oh, honey. I'm sorry to hear that. I'll go get your pie.

If you need to talk, I'm told I have great ears."

By the time Granger arrived, ten minutes later, Douglas had become so lost in thought, and the room had become so noisy, he hadn't realized anyone stood there until the man cleared his throat.

"Sergeant, it's nice to hear you. I've already ordered. Would you like something? I recommend the apple pie."

"Oh no, not for me. I have enough trouble keeping my weight down. I could really go for some coffee, though."

"Ruby should be back shortly. She'll get your coffee for you. It's really good here, not like the dishwater I often get in New York."

As if on cue, the waitress returned to Abledan's table, gently setting two dishes down.

"Coffee?" Sure. Coming right up."

"Listen, Mr. Abledan," Granger began. "I'm afraid I have some rather disturbing news about your friend."

"That's what you said when you called. Why do you suppose the police are always the conveyers of bad news, Sergeant? No, don't bother answering that."

Granger cleared his throat again. "I'm sorry to have to be the one to tell you, but I did some checking with the detective in charge of your friend's case. He wasn't very forthcoming, which is my problem not yours, but he did tell me she was murdered. Poisoned."

Douglas covered his face with his hands for a few minutes. When he looked up again, he wasn't sure how to continue.

"Did your detective know anything else? Has he any clues as to who might have done this?"

"He said the particular poison came from a plant called

Pennyroyal, but, I'm sorry to say, that's all the information he would give me. As I said, he isn't the most forthcoming person in the world. He's a very by-the-book kind of cop. He and I have had our problems about that over the years."

"I see. So I won't be able to get any more information about why Cara died or even who to blame for her death, will I?"

"Not from direct channels in a timely way anyway, I'm afraid. However, while you're in town, if I can be of any further assistance please feel free to contact me. Not being directly involved in the case, I'm not sure how much information I can acquire, but I am more willing than some to give you what I can."

"Thank you, Sergeant. I don't plan to leave town until I know what happened, even if I have to do some of the legwork on my own."

"I'd recommend not getting in the way of official police business."

"Don't worry about that, Sergeant."

"What I mean is, I may have inadvertently made your life a bit harder."

Douglas stared at the other man through his sightless eyes.

"You see, I told the detective you were the victim's boyfriend. It was a mistake to tell him, and I'm sorry. In my business, that makes you a prime suspect."

"I suppose it does. So you consider me a suspect as well then?"

"I can't exactly explain why, not without sounding like a jerk and a bigot, but no, I don't think you're involved, not in that way at least."

"Well, thank you for that. So, what you're saying is this detective will be investigating me?"

"Yes and, as I said, I am very sorry to have accidentally put you in this predicament."

"It will make my stay in Chicago less comfortable, and probably make finding out anything about Cara's death much more difficult, but I forgive you. He might have come across my name at some point anyway. Now, if you'll excuse me, I have things I must do. Have a good night, Sergeant."

* * *

When he arrived home, Granger felt both drained and upset. His job required him to inform people of the death of a loved one many times in the past. This time felt very different, perhaps because Abledan was alone in a strange city, or because he told Harris Abledan was the victim's boyfriend, therefore making him a suspect in the detective's mind. But, more likely, it was because the man was blind. He might have been called prejudiced for thinking so, but in his mind the blindness made him needier.

As he walked through the doorway, opposing sounds filled his ears. To the left, he heard his wife in the kitchen. Water running. Dishes clinking together. To the right, over the din of a television turned much too loud in the den, Kelly and Oskar argued about what to watch. Granger looked at his watch and smiled with relief. When the show ended they'd both go to bed and he'd share some quiet time with Tosha.

He walked to the kitchen, standing in the doorway for a

moment to watch his wife. She was beautiful, as beautiful as when he'd first met her. More so, if possible. He walked over to her, gently kissed her neck, and picked up a towel to dry the dishes laying beside the sink.

"You're late, Bubbala," she told him, trying to appear stern. "You said you would be home for dinner. The kids and I waited, but you know how they get when they're hungry. It isn't pretty."

"I'm sorry, Tosha, honey. After my shift I met with a man to tell him about the death of his girlfriend."

She stretched up on her toes so she could look into his eyes, then put her arms around his neck.

To her friends and family she went by the name Lydia, but, in the 11 years since they'd met, Granger had always called her Tosha. It was her middle name, but he thought it suited her better. And, like now, when she seemed to be in a playful mood, it allowed him to call her Tushie.

"Aren't there other people who could do that?"

"This was a special case. I met this man during that sewage leak downtown. He's from out of town, and blind, so I drove him back to his hotel and we talked about her. I told him I'd help him, if I could."

"That was sweet of you," she said, accenting the words with a soft kiss. "You look tired. Are you okay?"

"No. This case has really gotten to me. I don't know why, but it has. The woman was poisoned."

"What a horrible way to die."

"He wants to know why she was murdered and by whom, of course, but the detective in charge is more worried about following procedure than he is about really helping. It's Paul Harris. You remember the trouble I had with him a few years back, over another murder investigation?"

The skin on Tosha's forehead wrinkled, a sign Granger knew meant irritation.

"I remember. That was bad. I thought you'd lose your job over it. If Harris is involved you have to be careful, honey."

"I plan to be. He tried to goad me into an argument, but I didn't take the bait."

"*A feier zol im trefen,*" she said in a low voice.

"Tosha, I love you. But, you know cursing him to burn in hell, even when you say it in Yiddish, won't help matters."

The muscles in her forehead loosened, the redness in her cheeks faded. She giggled.

"I know, but it makes me feel better. There has to be some way you can help this man and also follow the procedures Harris wants you to. The one thing I remember you telling me about Paul Harris is he doesn't like to feel like anyone is doing an end-run around him, and he doesn't like short cuts."

"I know. And you know my philosophy. Sometimes shortcuts are necessary. We've talked about this before, Tosha. Don't worry. I can handle Harris."
The assurance was for Tosha's sake. Granger didn't know if he believed it himself.

# CHAPTER TEN
*Day 8*

Harris climbed underneath the yellow police tape surrounding the alley behind Capone's, groaning when his back complained from the effort. Dirt and debris, including a turned over trashcan and a pile of newspapers, cut gashes of shadow into the space. In one corner a family of rats busily labored on a new nest.

*This is a health code violation waiting to happen.*

The body itself lay on top of a pile of trash bags, as if it were to be simply picked up by the garbage collector in the morning. The woman was coatless, which seemed strange for this time of year, and her metallic, red dress had been pushed above her waist. Her legs were spread apart. Her pink, silken panties were wrapped around one ankle.

A young African-American man, whom Harris recognized as Ed Grimes, Dr. Hills's assistant in the coroner's office, circled around her, snapping pictures every few minutes from a different angle.

*Apparently he's more than just a lab tech.*

Bending over her body, Harris noted the victim's youth and beauty. Her golden hair splayed out around a cherublike face. Her skin, which probably glowed with life energy, now appeared dull and waxy.

*What's happening in this city? This was a human being, not some toy for a nut to get his jollies with before tossing in the trash.*

Harris shivered. If his wife were ever attacked and discarded like this he'd go on a rampage ending only when the scumbag lay at his feet eviscerated. He looked up and rubbed his eyes before focusing them on Hills. The man stood several feet away from the body, carefully watching his apprentice. He looked tired and bedraggled.

"So, Doctor, what do you make of this? Pretty disgusting, if you ask me."

"No one should be left alone to die in conditions such as these. I'll have to wait to do a full autopsy in the lab, of course, but what I can tell you is she was about twenty-five years old. No apparent scars, surgical or otherwise. No tattoos or other identifying marks. Judging from her body temperature, and the degree of rigor mortis, she's been dead from seven to ten hours. As you can see, the local vermin took a few bits out of her face and arms before she was discovered. There's a wide, deep depression along her throat, indicating she'd been strangled. Young Edward has taken some good pictures. They should tell us something, and I'll know more after my work-up. Oh, one more thing. She did not die here."

Harris raised an eyebrow. "Oh?"

"I found scuff marks on the back of her shoes. And the body had time to sit for a while where the murder took place. Blood pooled in places it would not have if she died here. Her body was dragged to this pile of garbage."

"Thank you, Doctor."

Two uniformed officers, one of them feverishly writing on a small pad, stood at Capone's rear entrance with a man in a dark business suit. Harris flashed his badge and identified himself, then pulled his voice recorder from his pocket and switched it on.

"This is the night manager of Capone's," the taller of the two officers said, "Carl Bruckner. The victim's name is Lucy Tanner. She's worked as a waitress in the restaurant for the past three years."

"What can you tell me about Miss Tanner," Harris asked, as he quickly took in small details, like the squint in the man's eye, which made him suspicious. "What kind of employee was she? Did she flirt with customers? Anyone she might have attracted or pissed off?"

"I didn't know her well, and, to tell you the truth, we didn't get along very well. She's been a good enough worker, but something about her bothered me. It wasn't anything I could put my finger on, just the kind of feeling you sometimes get about some people who rub you the wrong way. You know."

"So, you didn't like her. Did it go further than that?" Harris winked.

Brucker's dark eyes opened wide. He grunted. "No, nothing like that. She was an employee, nothing more. And I'm not attracted to twenty-something women anyway."

"Did she have any love interests among the staff that you know of? Someone who might have been jealous or upset with her?"

"I don't get involved in the personal lives of the staff, Detective. That's frowned upon by the owners, and it's bad for business. But I can tell you that one of our customers came to see her this afternoon. He wanted to talk to her about his girlfriend. After he left, I found Lucy crying."

"Who was this guy? What did he look like?"

"I didn't get his name. But, he was about five foot seven, had longish blonde hair, and carried one of those sonic cane things."

"Sonic canes?"

"Yeah. Cause, you know, he was blind."

*Abledan.* "Did she tell you why she was crying, or what he said to her?

"As I said before, he spoke to her about his girlfriend and about the drink Lucy had served her when they'd come in earlier. An Old Fashioned, if I remember correctly. I'm sorry, but that's all I recall."

Harris began to walk away when Bruckner cleared his throat. "I don't know if it's important, Detective, but now that I think about it, there was also a woman who came by to talk to Lucy, if you can call it talking. It was a very angry conversation."

"You didn't happen to hear what they were arguing about, did you?"

"I don't make a habit of listening in on other people's conversations."

"That doesn't mean you didn't hear anything, does it? Without really listening, I mean."

"Well, they were accusing each other of stealing the other's boyfriend. In fact, it got so nasty the woman had to be escorted off the premises. But, not before she pulled out a handful of Lucy's hair."

Harris snapped off the recorder. Clearly this wasn't going to be a cut and dry case. Abledan was involved somehow, and he was determined to find out how.

* * *

Joshua Dorn sat on the couch in his living room when the local news came on TV. The sound was turned low, but, when Cordelia's picture appeared next to the reporter, he put down his coffee and picked up the remote.

"Our top story this morning," the announcer said, "is the death of a local, prominent scientist. Dr. Cara Cordelia, head of the agricultural pathology department at Cornell University, was attending a conference in Chicago when she suffered convulsions and died suddenly. Neither police nor officials at the University of Illinois, where the conference was being held, were available for comment. The cause of Dr. Cordelia's death has yet to be determined."

Dorn smiled. It was finally over. He wouldn't have to listen to her whining and prattling anymore. Her work wouldn't threaten to cause any more damage either. Now, he only hoped Ortega could be trusted to keep the investigation away from him.

* * *

Researching Cordelia's murder presented Douglas with several problems, not the least of which was the technology involved. He wasn't at home, and didn't have access to his computer. Though wearable computers were becoming more and more popular by the day, he could never scrape together enough money to afford one suitable for a blind user. They were considered specialty items and, as such, were hugely expensive.

The only alternative available to him, find a local computer with an Internet connection. Easy enough to do. A library or Internet cafe would supply the hardware.

Software, however, would definitely be an issue. His home computer held specially designed programs for blind users; voice recognition, and a reader which translated text on the screen into spoken words. He might be able to find those kinds of software, but he doubted another computer would have the security protocols he'd installed. And since, in a library or cafe he wouldn't be behind a firewall, anyone who wanted to could have access to the research he planned on conducting. That was a major concern.

At home, he could hack into a police computer with reasonable certainty he would avoid detection. Not here. At home, he could do searches that might otherwise send up red flags on law-enforcement computers. He had done those kind of searches before and not gotten caught. Here though, he'd have to be more careful in his wording. Looking up the effects of poisons in this post-9/11 world could draw attention. Still, he had to take the risk if he wanted to find answers. He finished dressing, then made his way to the library.

* * *

"Here we are," a young woman said, after guiding Douglas to a private room in the back of the library. "We only have one computer set up for someone with your needs. We had another, but it's out being updated. This machine has a fairly rudimentary speech database, but it should be sufficient for most needs. Just say 'wake up' when you're ready. There's a Braille printer to your left, if you need a hard copy of anything. I'll leave you alone now. Use the intercom if you need anything further."

Douglas slid onto a plastic chair, shifting his weight before settling into a comfortable position, then began what he expected would be a long conversation with the computer. He asked a series of questions, which were answered by a harsh electronic voice.

"Historically," the computer began, "Pennyroyal has been used in a variety of ways. In British history the whole herb was often used as a deterrent to fleas and other pests. During the reign of Henry VIII it was sewn into fur collars worn by the royal court. Until 1915, some thought of it as a restorative and brewed it as a tea. Both Native American medicine men and the more modern medical community offered it as a quick abortive to pregnant women, though it often caused the death of both mother and fetus. The natives also used it as a means of slow torture and death for captured enemies.

Pennyroyal comes in two varieties, American (Hedeoma Pulgeioides) and European (Mentha Pulegium). Both are highly toxic, with the European variety being more potent. The plant is distinguished by small, oval leaves arranged opposite each other on a square stem. The leaves may be sparsely-toothed or smooth on the margins. The stems grow erect, up to one foot in height, from a many-branched root system. The tiny blue-violet flowers grow in whorls from the leaf axils on the top half of the stems. The oil, when distilled, carries eighty-five to ninety- two percent of the toxin, Pulegone. The oil has a very sweet aroma and minty flavor. Its coloration can range from clear to pale green or lavender.

The toxic effects of Pulegone are cumulative. Three tablespoons of the substance is enough to cause death.

Symptoms include nausea, vomiting, abdominal pain, diarrhea, excessive sweating, chills, headache, dizziness, extreme thirst, muscle spasms, hallucinations, drowsiness, fatigue, confusion, seizures, organ failure, elevated heart rate, elevated blood pressure, reduced blood sugar, loss of consciousness, and death. There is no known antidote."

Douglas sat at the computer for a few minutes, letting a mixture of anger, sadness, and surprise wash over him.

*What a horrible way to die. Who would do such a thing? Why?*

* * *

Back at his hotel, Douglas picked up the phone and asked the automated voice to connect him with Delta Airlines. After waiting on the line for twenty minutes, while music and 'travel specials' reminders blared in his ear, a human voice answered. He explained he was looking for one of their flight attendants.

"We were both on flight sixteen forty-four, New York to Chicago, on September seventeenth."

"May I ask what this is in reference to, Mr. Abledan? We aren't supposed to put our customers in contact with our flight crew staff."

"I understand that. Let me explain. I'm a blind man, and this was my first flight since losing my vision. I was, admittedly, rather nervous about the experience. Your staff was particularly helpful to me, especially the flight attendant. She made me feel very comfortable and attended to my specific needs. I wanted to personally thank her for her help."

None of this was a lie. Douglas meant everything he just said, but it was not the reason he wanted to speak with the woman. Of course, the person he was now speaking with didn't need to know his real intent. He doubted he'd get very far with her if he explained he wanted to discuss the aroma of a particular cup of tea with the flight attendant.

"I understand what you're saying, Mr. Abledan, and I appreciate your desire to speak to the individual directly. As a representative for the airline, I can assure you we try very hard to accommodate the needs of our passengers, especially those who require special attention. I'm pleased to hear this particularly flight attendant was as courteous and helpful as you needed her to be. However, I must repeat, it is against airline policy to put customers in direct contact with staff members. Even if that had not always been the policy, security measures initiated after the September eleventh attacks strengthened the airline's resolve to enforce the no-contact rules. You can understand, I'm sure, we have no way of knowing a customer's true motivations for desiring such contact information."

Of course he did understand the need for such policies to exist. And, overall, they made sense. But Douglas could not allow such a generalized policy to stop him from speaking to this particular flight attendant about the specific incident for which he needed information. To that end, he continued to make his case to several members of the airline hierarchy until finally he decided the only way he would get the information he required was by divulging his true motivation.

"I'm a private investigator. I'm working in conjunction with the Chicago Police Department on a murder investigation that might involve members of your staff."

This wasn't a lie either. Sergeant Granger did know he was talking to people, asking questions about Cordelia's death. And Granger was a member of the Chicago police department so, in a sense he was working in conjunction with, or at least with the knowledge of, the police.

"You could have said so from the beginning, Detective."

* * *

With the name of the flight attendant and her schedule in hand, Douglas took a cab to the airport. He remembered the woman had a lovely Japanese accent. He would enjoy hearing it again. But, he had to remember, his main purpose was to get information from her. There had been something strange about the aroma of the tea the stewardess served, or so he remembered thinking at the time. Now, in hindsight, he wondered whether the drink had been poisoned. It would have been a perfect opportunity, but it was only one of several he knew of. He had not spent a lot of time with Cordelia while in Chicago. She could have been exposed to many opportunities he wasn't privy to. With only this one piece of the puzzle in hand it would be difficult to find her murderer, but what choice did he have. He owed it to her, or at least felt like he did. There was also the other piece of information Granger gave him. The main detective on the case suspected him. Investigating the case himself, therefore, was in his own interest.

Douglas was once again surrounded by noise. To his left, a man harangued a woman about misplaced tickets. To his right a group of bored children played a noisy game of tag. His sonic cane vibrated constantly as he circumvented one obstacle after another. The vibration was almost a noise in itself and interpreting the signal added to the raucous symphony threatening to distract him from the task at hand.

As he approached the Delta gate where he was told the woman would be arriving, a list of questions flooded into his mind. Had she noticed anything peculiar about Cordelia, something she could see that he couldn't? Had she noticed anything odd about the aroma of the tea? Had she used the sealed teabag Cordelia handed her? He hoped the woman would be as cooperative and helpful as she had been during the flight.

It turned out his timing could not have been better. Passengers had just disembarked at the gate. He walked into the path of the nearest one.

"Excuse me, I'm trying to find a young woman, the flight attendant that took care of me on flight sixteen forty-four a few days ago. Her name is Elizabeth Ito. I was told she'd be on this plane."

"Oh yeah," a young woman replied. "I was supposed to work that flight, but Liz called to ask if I'd switch with her. She said she needed the extra hours. Personally, I think she wanted to spend time with someone."

"How do you know that?"

"She kept talking about a woman a friend wanted her to meet. It sounded like the guy really wanted her to hook up. Funny thing is, we're really tight, and I never got the impression she swung that way. She's never talked about other women, not in that way. Anyhow, I've got to go. Please, don't say anything about our chat. Liz would be really upset with me. She's on cleanup detail on this plane, so she should be coming out soon. Oh, there she is. I'll let her know you're looking for her."

* * *

A moment passed. Then, a soft voice asked how she could help him. He recognized the accent immediately.

"Miss Ito? I'm glad I found you. I don't know if you remember me. My name is Douglas Abledan. We were on flight sixteen forty-four, from New York, on September seventeenth together. I was seated next to a woman who asked you to brew a cup of tea for her."

"I'm sorry, Mr. Abledan, I don't remember. I serve a lot of tea."

The tone of the woman's voice, in that one sentence, spoke volumes. She was lying, and nervous about doing so. Douglas needed to find out why.

"This particular tea had a very sweet aroma. My friend had brought her own bag. It was peppermint, but it did not smell like peppermint after you poured the water over the bag. The thing is, Miss Ito, Cara died two days after we arrived here in Chicago."

"I'm terribly sorry for your loss, Mr. Abledan."

"Thank you. I'm trying to find out if her death was due to anything she might have been allergic to. People have allergic reactions to many things, and sometimes they die from it. When I was younger, I learned sometimes these sensitivities take time to build up. A person might not show any ill effects when they are first exposed to something they eat or drink. Sometime later though, when they are exposed again, they have a reaction. That happened to me.

Fortunately, my doctor caught it in time and treated me. I'm not trying to blame anyone. But, I'm sure you can understand, I simply must know what happened."

"I don't know how I can help you. Frankly, I don't remember you or your friend and, as I said, I serve a lot of tea to passengers. Now, I don't mean to seem rude or insensitive, but I have to go."

Without another word, the woman rushed past him. Something Douglas said had spooked her. Suddenly a switch clicked in his mind and he realized he'd uncovered a connection to the poison that had killed Cordelia. He didn't know where this new piece of information fit, but nothing would stop him from finishing the puzzle.

* * *

Elizabeth Tuttle never saw Ortega read by lamplight before. Under its glow, his soft age lines became deep valleys. As he poured over each page of the notes she'd given him, the intensity of his concentration increased. It frightened her. Finally, after almost an hour, he raised his head and stared at her with a look threatening to peer into her soul.

"What is that noise? That scratching sound. Do you hear it?"

"A nervous habit of mine," Tuttle said, flinching at the abruptness of his voice. She lifted the three stones from her pocket. "Rubbing these helps me when I'm nervous. I like the sound and the weight of them."

"What do you mean? Are you nervous, Doctor?"

"No, 'nesto...Dr. Ortega," she lied. "I'm not nervous

when I'm with you."

"Then stop playing with those damned rocks."

Sheepishly, the woman pushed her hand back into her pocket, letting the stones fall into the fold of cloth.

"Listen, are you sure no one else read these notes? Are you positive?"

"I can't be positive, but the pages appeared to be untouched."

"And you made sure your forgeries were perfect? No one will suspect anything?"

"I've been practicing her handwriting for a long time. I've even replaced some of her memos from time to time, as a kind of test. No one notices the difference."

Ortega grimaced. This woman took unnecessary risks more often than he would have liked.

"I trust you made no copies, either of Cordelia's notes or the forgeries."

"Of course not. What would be the purpose? Any copies could be linked to me. We wouldn't want that, would we? As far as anyone knows Dr. Cordelia was my friend."

"Excellent, then the corn plague will continue, just as Gaia ordained."

Ortega looked at the papers once more before pushing them back into the folder. Turning to the wall behind his desk, he removed a framed photograph to reveal a safe. He placed his thumb in the center of the metal door, waited a moment until the tumblers clicked into place, then secured the folder inside. When he switched off the desk lamp, and closed his eyes, Tuttle knew she'd been dismissed.

* * *

Harris sat at his desk listening to the notes he'd dictated about the Cordelia case. The only lead he had so far was that she apparently had a boyfriend in Chicago, someone none of her colleagues, not even her friend, Elizabeth Tuttle, knew anything about. That seemed very strange to
say the least. He picked up the phone and, before the recorded voice had a chance to interrogate him, asked to be connected to the Agricultural School at Cornell University in Ithaca, New York.

After a few seconds, Harris was treated to soft guitar music, reminding him of an old song he'd once heard played by a Jose Feliciano impersonator. His body relaxed for the first time in days. His mind drifted, and he saw his wife, Alice, sitting with him in a nightclub in California. A sudden voice on the other end of the line broke the illusion.

"Joshua Dorn here. May I help you?"

"I'm Detective Paul Harris, with the Chicago Police Department. I'm sorry to inform you, but Dr. Cara Cordelia has died."

The line fell silent for a moment. "I was Dr. Cordelia's assistant. I heard about her death on the news. Very tragic. We're all terribly upset about it. How did she die? She seemed in good health when she left here."

"We're not sure what the cause of death was," Harris lied. "But I can tell you her death was apparently relatively quick and painless." Another lie. "Your office was the only contact information we could acquire. Did she have any family? Anyone we can contact?"

"Not that I am aware of, Detective."

"Okay. You're it then. Can you tell me if she had any

physical complaints before leaving New York?"

"She was tired, and worried about the conference. She had been working around the clock lately, trying to identify a very elusive pathogen."

"I know about her work. Something to do with the corn plague, if I remember correctly."

"I'm sure you've spoken to other conference attendees by now, Detective, so you know she had the enviable task of identifying the new pathogen. It was very exciting work, and I felt honored assisting her on the project."

Harris hated phone interviews. He had trouble hearing vocal inflections despite the supposedly "crystal clear" connection, and he didn't like the absence of the body language that often gave him so much information. To make matters worse, Dorn seemed to be even more guarded than most people.

"I'm sure it was. So, except for fatigue, there was no sign anything was wrong with her? Can you think of anyone who might want to harm her? Someone who might have been jealous of her, perhaps?"

This was a tricky question. Harris didn't want to create the suspicion of murder in Dorn's mind, but the answer might provide him with a lead to cracking the case, something he sorely needed.

"As I said, discovery of a new virus is an enviable pursuit, but I can't think of any other researcher who would do her harm simply out of jealousy. She was both well-liked and highly respected in her field."

"I see. Do you know anything about her boyfriend, a man named Douglas Abledan?"

"A boyfriend?" Dorn asked, clearly thrown by the

question. "I think you have the wrong woman in mind. To my knowledge, Dr. Cordelia didn't give herself much time for any sort of a social life. She was a dedicated scientist. Driven, you might say. We're under a lot of pressure here, as I'm sure you can imagine, but I tried to tell her she needed to get out more often. I'm sorry to say my suggestions fell on deaf ears."

Was Abledan lying? It wouldn't be the first time a suspect harbored delusions of a relationship that did not really exist. Harris would have to delve deeper into his story.

"It would appear she did listen to you, at least somewhat. She was seen in a Chicago restaurant with a man who doesn't seem to have been a colleague."

Harris smacked his forehead. He'd made a rookie mistake. Scientists dealt in absolutes and they loved to test hypotheses. He hoped Dorn wasn't so interested in his boss's love life he'd look into the matter.

"No one knows everything there is to know about their employers, Detective. I know about Dr. Cordelia's work, of course, but little else. Was this man involved somehow in her death?"

Harris ignored the question, thanked Dorn for his time, and slammed down the phone. The interview hadn't given him any solid leads, but it had given him cause to watch Abledan, closely.

* * *

Harris spent the afternoon at the university, interviewing the scientists. He wasn't happy. Somehow being around "eggheads" always made him feel diminished. He was an educated man. In fact, he had half of a law degree. But, people like these academics always seemed superior in some way. He hated the feeling, and wasn't entirely sure where it came from, but he couldn't shake it.

Speaking with Ortega only made him feel worse. The guy was smug, not to mention arrogant. But, and this made matters worse, he had been correct. Harris didn't understand half of what he'd said. Murder, was easy to understand. You have a victim, a perpetrator, and a motive. The challenge lay in linking them altogether. For the most part it was an interesting challenge too, until complications arose. Unfortunately this case, which had started out so simply, was becoming complicated. Clearly, Ortega was not going to be cooperative, despite his protestations to the contrary. To make matters worse the beat cop, Granger, was breaking the rules again and giving out classified information.

"Dammit!"

"Excuse me, Detective?"

Harris refocused his attention toward the man sitting on the other side of the table. Dr. Lad Dawson, a young man, with a slight build and dark, brown hair, reminded Harris of the son he once had. Ray would have been about the same age this man appeared to be, if he had lived.

Against departmental policy, Harris had taken his ten-year-old son on a drive-along. He had been paying for it ever since. The crash, involving a drunk driver in an old SUV without a navigator device, caused him to spend a month in the hospital and it cost Ray his life. Harris closed his eyes for a moment, collecting his thoughts. He had to keep those images out of his mind. Murder investigations needed to be emotionless.

"Nothing. So, Dr. Dawson, you were telling me about your work."

"I was just saying I'm a geneticist. I create gene therapies which help crops maintain their resistance to parasitic organisms."

"And how does that relate to this conference?"

"Well, the organism attacking the corn crops is parasitic in nature, meaning it needs a host plant in order to propagate."

Harris rolled his eyes. "That's very interesting. Tell me, does your work ever involve poisonous plants?"

Dawson shifted his weight. The question had the desired effect. It had, literally, thrown the scientist off balance.

"What I mostly do is make crops 'taste bad' to parasites so they won't be attacked by them."

Something in the man's voice told Harris there was more to his story. He knew more than he was saying.

"I see. Did you know Dr. Cordelia?"

"I've read several of her papers, of course. She was quite brilliant, you know. And, we'd met a few times at conferences, but I wouldn't say I knew her. We were colleagues doing similar research. That's all."

"I see. Then you wouldn't know anything about a man she was socializing with?"

"A man? No. I don't have the time, or the inclination for that matter, to delve into the social lives of my colleagues. I'm here to do a job, to help find a cure for this disease. That's all. If Dr. Cordelia had time to have a man in her life, good for her."

*Another dead end.* "Well, thank you, Doctor. That will be all, for now."

* * *

Armed with an understanding of the poison that killed Cordelia, Douglas now needed to find out who might have been capable of distilling and using it. The first person he thought of calling was Ernesto Ortega, the man he'd met at the dojo who'd said he was an administrator at the university.

Ortega hadn't seemed overly disturbed by Cordelia's death, which was strange in and of itself, but he had knowledge Douglas needed to tap into. It was quite possible speaking with him, or the other researchers, would put another link in the chain leading to the murderer.

Douglas pushed as hard as he dared during their conversation, but found Ortega oddly reticent, going as far as to suggest, instead of speaking to the researchers, Douglas's "investigation" would be better served by a contact with the police.

"I've been led to believe getting information from the police would be difficult at best," he said. "And, even if I could, it would mean wading through a mountain of red tape. My boss is already breathing down my neck about getting back to work. I can't afford to waste my time dealing with bureaucracy. Frankly, one of your people might be able to give me insight about who Cara was, from a professional point of view. I don't mean to accuse anyone, but that might tell me if a colleague could be compelled to murder her."

"I can assure you none of my staff would feel so

'compelled,' Douglas. And, I must tell you, I am rather insulted by your insinuation. But, if you are so determined to follow this line of reasoning, then I suppose I can't stop you. I will inform the staff and the visiting dignitaries you'll be coming."

The phone line died with a bang.

* * *

Douglas was in no mood for visitors when he heard a sharp rap on the door. But, shaking his head, he unlocked and pulled it open.

"Douglas Abledan?" The voice was thick and husky. "I'm Detective Paul Harris. May I come in? I have a few questions to ask you about Dr. Cara Cordelia."

Douglas knew he had no choice in the matter. Sergeant Granger warned him to expect a visit from this man, and his tone suggested he was not an easy person to put off. But, with luck, he'd be able to use the interview to his advantage. Any new information he could learn about Cordelia's murder, would be beneficial.

"Of course, Detective. Please, come in. I was told you might be stopping by."

"It seems you made quite an impression with one of my officers."

"Sergeant Granger has been very helpful."

Without asking permission, Harris pulled his recorder from his coat pocket and switched it on. The click of the switch resonated in Douglas's ears, but he chose to ignore it.

"Then, you know why I'm here. I'm looking into Dr. Cordelia's death. I understand you were in a relationship with her. Can you tell me how long you've been seeing each other?"

Douglas thought for several seconds. He needed to tell the truth, but he also realized doing so might land him in trouble, not to mention what it would do to his investigation.

"I'm not sure I understand you, Detective."

Harris snorted. "It's a simple enough question. Were you together for years? Months? Weeks?"

"Well, to be totally honest, it seemed a lot longer than it actually was. We grew very close, very quickly."

Harris leaned forward. "Evasion is not always the best part of valor, Mr. Abledan, especially when speaking to the police. I'm going to go out on a limb here and suggest you've been lying. You weren't really in a relationship with her, were you?"

Douglas ran his hand through his hair. "Well, umm, if you put it that way I'd have to say no, but I was quite attracted to her. Given time, I'd like to think the kind of relationship you're speaking of would have developed."

"That's very sweet, but pipedreams aside, I could arrest you for interfering with an investigation."

"You could, except I'm not interfering. I'm simply doing my own footwork."

"I've seen your type many times, Abledan." You're a glory seeker. You want the world to see you as a hero."

Douglas shook his head. "No, you don't understand." *I don't trust you to find her murderer.*

"Then, please, explain it to me. Please tell me why you've been asking so many questions, pretending to be something you're not so you can prey on people's sympathies."

Douglas felt the question like a wave slamming against the shore. The muscles in his neck locked. His teeth mashed together. It took effort to keep his face relaxed.

"It's sort of a hobby of mine. I don't mean to do it, but somehow I find myself involved in these things."

"You mean murders," Harris said, in a low voice. "You get involved in murders? How many times have you done this?"

Douglas explained that, due to a glitch in his navigator, he had accidentally been "present" at the murder of John P. Haggarty, the president of Unimat Corporation, and, using the technology, he helped the New York City police solve the crime.

Harris grunted. "Are you trying to tell me you *stumbled* onto a murder?"

"I have to tell you, I'm not pleased with your tone, Detective. If you doubt what I'm saying, that's fine. But, before you make up your mind I'm some sort of thrill seeker, or worse a murderer, might I suggest you speak to a Detective named Henkle at the 88th precinct in New York City? We didn't exactly get along well, but I'm sure he will explain who I am and what the circumstances of my involvement were."

"You can be sure I'll check out your story, Mr. Abledan."

The statement sounded like a threat, one that, determined to make his point, Douglas ignored.

"Anyway, if I had not stumbled onto the murder it would have been written off as a drug related drive-by shooting. New York gets so many of those they're often ignored. The investigation wouldn't have gone further than that. Believe me. I've seen it happen before. But that's why I'm here. I needed to get away. People kept asking me questions. It got so bad I couldn't concentrate at work. Then I met Dr. Cordelia on the plane coming to Chicago. When I heard she died I felt as if I should find out how and why."

"I see. So, you only met her on the plane? You didn't see her at all while you've been here?"

"Actually, I did. We had dinner together."

"When?"

Douglas pursed his lips. His eyebrows rose slightly. "This won't sound good, but it was the night before she died."

"You're right. That is awkward."

"It was a short night, though. After dinner Cara became ill. I put her in a cab and sent her back to her hotel."

"Where did you eat?"

"I think the place was called Capone's. A twenty's-style nightclub a few blocks from here."

"And that was the last time you saw her?"

Douglas frowned. "Sadly. I wish that hadn't been the case, I assure you. She was a lovely woman, in many ways."

"So, let me get this straight. You only saw her twice and yet you still decided to 'do some legwork' regarding her death? And you insinuated yourself into the investigation by calling yourself her boyfriend?"

"I already explained my reasoning to you. I'm sure you would have done the same thing."

Harris grumbled. "I would have left it to the professionals, and that's what I expect you to do from this point forward."

Douglas heard a sharp click coming from about

waist level. Whatever it was Harris had turned on when he'd first arrived, he just switched it off. Without another word he stormed out of the hotel room, leaving Douglas to wonder both how much trouble he was in, and how much of a nuisance Harris would be. Regardless, he wouldn't be curtailing his investigation.

# CHAPTER ELEVEN

"Luiz, you have to go to Chicago."

"Have to, Joan? Why? That idiot, Ortega, said he didn't want my help."

"You'd do the same thing. Your pride would get in the way, I'm sure of it. Didn't you tell me Dr. Cordelia said she thought your work was important?"

"Don't you think they can figure this out on their own?"

"Maybe, but we were there, Luiz. You know as well as I do how this whole thing started. It could help if they knew also."

"That's exactly my point. They don't know how it started. They don't know it was our fault. Aren't we in enough trouble with Ramirez and the university? Do we really need more?"

"I was just trying to stop you from making a mistake, that's all. How could I know stopping you from doing something both selfish and stupid would cause this kind of trouble?"

"Neither of us knew it, Joan."

"That's true. But what we do know is you have the training and expertise that might stop the disease from spreading any further. I love you, Luiz. Please do this, for both of us. We're trying to make a life for ourselves. What would that matter if this disease spreads and the whole world suffers from it?"

Garcia thought for a moment. This could work out to be a very good thing. If he went to Chicago he might get his name in the archeology textbooks. Certainly he'd be able to get the respect he was due, which would virtually guarantee Joan the kind of life she deserved.

Walking over to the closet, Aquilla took out a large, black, woven suitcase and opened it.

"I've already made a reservation for you for this afternoon. You'd best start packing." She kissed Garcia gently on the lips and left the room, her long, raven hair trailing like a bird's plume behind her.

* * *

"Mr....Abledan, is it?"

"Thank you for seeing me, Dr. Tuttle. I know you're very busy."

"Please, don't think twice about it. I'm told you were Cara's friend. Funny, she never mentioned you."

"We hadn't been together very long."

"I see. Well, I'm sorry for your loss."

"Thank you. Dr. Ortega tells me you two were close."

"I've known Cara for about a year now. We hit it off right away. We only saw each other at conferences, like this one, but we talked on the phone all the time. At first, it was strictly business, you know, pathology and agriculture. Then, as we got to know each other better, I guess we both relaxed a bit and found we had a lot in common. It didn't take long for us to become good friends. I'll miss her."

Something seemed familiar about this woman. After a moment's thought, Douglas recognized what it was. An aroma he'd smelled before. But where? After another moment he knew. He'd first noticed it in the tea the airline stewardess served Cordelia. Then, it appeared in the drink the waitress at Capone's served. Another piece of the puzzle fell into place, but his instincts told him he couldn't let this woman suspect he'd made the connection. However, he'd be certain to tell Granger.

"What can you tell me about Cara? Anything I might not know? You've known her much longer than I have, and in a completely different environment. I'm trying to find out why someone would have killed her."

"I wish I knew. Well, to answer your question, I'm sure I don't have to tell you she was brilliant, or that she was totally dedicated to her work. I could call her late at night from home and she would still be in her office doing some research or other. I liked that about her, her dedication. When she allowed herself downtime she liked to read science fiction, the old stories from the 1950's. I never got into that stuff, though she'd loaned me a few books. She was funny too. She could tell a joke with the best of them. She minded the raunchy stuff though. Not like me. I don't mind a dirty joke, but she was an old-school girl. Some things just didn't sit right with her. Profanity was one of those things. That could be an age thing. I'm only twenty- nine, you know."

Douglas was surprised. The woman seemed far older than she'd said she was. Some women lied about their age, but this felt different. He felt she had experience, a history, that somehow felt sad.

"It didn't get in the way of our friendship. One thing struck me as funny when we first were hanging out together, though. She rarely drank. At conferences, a bunch of us would go out to dinner, to unwind from the long days, you know. I would ask her if she wanted to have a cocktail, or some wine. More often than not she turned me down. It was only recently I found out she was diabetic. I didn't think diabetics were supposed to drink alcohol at all. She liked sweet drinks too, and that surprised me."

Suddenly, the woman paused, and Douglas wondered whether she'd reached the end of her story, or if she'd decided she'd divulged some secret she wasn't supposed to mention. He nodded as the image of his friend, Tim, came to mind.

"I had a good friend in high school who was diabetic. He never said anything. I only found out years later, when his sister mentioned it."

His thoughts moved to Cordelia, to the dinner he'd shared with her at Capone's. The images he'd created in his mind were so strong he could almost smell her perfume. They'd had a lively conversation in which he'd demonstrated-perhaps too boldly, now that he thought about it-his ability to recognize music. But, shortly after she'd taken a sip of the drink with the strange aroma, she'd become ill. Now, he thought he might know why.

"I won't take up anymore of your time, Dr. Tuttle. Oh, but there is one more thing you can do for me. While I'm here I'd like to stop in and say hello to Dr. Ortega. Could you direct me to his office?"

There was an awkward pause, but before Douglas realized what was happening, the woman entwined his arm with hers.

"You know what. It'll be easier if I just take you there

myself."

They walked, arm-in-arm, through the twists and turns of the immense complex. Douglas realized he'd probably have gotten lost if he'd been by himself, even with good directions and his sonic cane as guides. Finally, they stopped and Tuttle disengaged herself from his arm.

"I'll leave you here. I've got to get back to my work now."

Douglas listened for Tuttle's fading footfalls, then knocked on the door in front of him, lightly enough to make sure his presence was noticed, but not too heavily to disturb Ortega if he was busy.

"Hello, Ernesto? It's Douglas Abledan."

When Ortega invited him in, Douglas pushed the heavy wooden door open, then closed it behind him, and walked into the room, almost bumping into a large object. The sonic cane couldn't tell him what it was but, given its presence in an office, he surmised the object was probably a desk.

"Hello, Ernesto," he said, extending his hand. "I was just speaking to one of your colleagues, a Dr. Tuttle, and thought I'd better stop in and say hello before I left."

After a moment, during which he felt his hand gripped tightly, Douglas noticed a faint odor in the room. It was subtle, probably too much so for most people to discern from what was always in the air. It smelled like warm copper, almost like coins that had been sitting in the sun for some period of time. He thought for a moment, then recognized the scent, blood.

"Did you cut yourself shaving this morning, Ernesto?"

"What an odd question. No. I shaved without incident this morning. Thank you. Why the concern?"

"There's a distinct aroma of blood in the air. It's faint, and I seriously doubt anyone but another blind man would notice it. But it is unmistakable."

Ortega inhaled sharply. "That's amazing! Last night I had a minor mishap at the dojo with one of the white belts, a young woman with rather long, sharp fingernails. Her hands slipped when she tried to throw me, and she scratched my arm. Though rather painful, and bloody, at the time, the wound has already begun to heal. I'm simply astonished you could smell the dried blood, especially with all the other scents in the building's air."

Douglas, suddenly becoming aware of the pungent scent of sweat, didn't answer immediately. Ortega was nervous, and probably lying. He didn't know why, but now was not the time to challenge him.

"It's a tradeoff. I lost my sight, but learned what different, usually unnoticed, things smell like."

"Very interesting. On a different note, tell me, did you learn anything from your chat with my staff?"

Douglas shook his head. "Not much. I learned a little more about Cara, from Dr. Tuttle. As you'd told me, they were good friends. But, unfortunately, there was nothing relevant to her death."

"I'm sorry we couldn't be more helpful," Ortega said, though to Douglas's ear the words sounded hollow.

* * *

Ortega watched on the security camera as Douglas left the building. Before he could turn back to his work, Elizabeth Tuttle knocked on the door, entering the room without waiting for a reply, a constantly annoying violation of edict.

"I think we need to talk. Someone came to see me about Cara, a friend of hers. He asked a lot of questions about my relationship with her. He wanted to know if I knew anything about her that he didn't."

"So, what did you tell him?"

"Don't worry, 'nesto. You know I only ever tell people what I think they need to know."

Ortega growled at the woman's constant informality. "Perhaps, but I think you sometimes say more than you should."

The woman shook her head. "I simply told him we had been friends for about a year. And, I thought she was a sweet and funny person."

"You have to be careful, Elizabeth. Abledan is a smart man. Smarter than I originally would have given him credit for. I let him come in to talk to the staff because no one besides you and I know anything he could use. I thought he would ask a few questions then drop the matter quickly. But, from your tone, it doesn't sound as though you think he was satisfied with what you said."

"You should have told me he would be coming. I would have been better prepared."

"I didn't want you 'prepared.' Some people can see through that. I think Abledan might be one of those people."

"Maybe. I don't think he really believed everything I was saying. I think he thought I was holding something back. And, of course, I was."

"I'll take care of it," Ortega said, turning to face the computer on his desk. "You'd better get back to your work now."

Once Tuttle left the room, Ortega dropped his pretense of aloofness. Leaning back in his chair, he pondered how he would handle the problem of Abledan. The man was blind, but still dangerous. He'd have to be dealt with, soon.

* * *

Nothing about Douglas's trip to the university felt right. Tuttle's scent was all too familiar, and the story Ortega told didn't gel. But, it occurred to him, at least Ortega's mishap could be verified with a phone call to the dojo. After a few minutes of idle conversation with Sensei Thomans about his own experiences, he asked about Ortega.

"I understand Ernesto was injured the last time he was in, and I wanted to make sure he was alright."

"Injured? No. Ortega never reported anything."

Thomans' answer wasn't a surprise. Ortega had been sweating when he told the story, and the room was anything but hot. After apologizing for the intrusion, and thanking Thomans for his help, Douglas put the phone down and laid back on the bed. Ernesto was hiding something, but what could it be? Some link in the chain he wasn't connecting? Whatever it was, it apparently led to Cordelia.

* * *

Harris sat at his desk staring at the phone. Asking for help on a case, especially from another department, especially New York, wasn't something he wanted to do. He had a history with New York, and it wasn't a good one. Those guys thought they owned the world, like every department in the world had to do whatever they wanted. And, if he must to be totally honest with himself, he hated sharing the credit of breaking a suspect with anyone. On the other hand, departmental policy obligated him to check out Abledan's story, no matter how farfetched it sounded. It was, however, an excruciatingly physical effort to pick up the phone.

His hand hovered over the receiver, as if the appendage was deciding for itself what it wanted to do. After a long moment, he snatched it up, barking into the mouthpiece.

The line rang twice before a digitized voice asked which precinct he wanted to be connected to.

"I forget the precinct number."

"Please repeat the precinct number," the voice said.

Harris strummed his fingers on the glass covering his desktop.

"I don't know the damned number."

"I'm sorry, I still don't understand. Please repeat the number of the precinct you'd like to be connected with."

Harris moaned, then realized he was sitting in front of his computer. Never having been computer savvy, he'd refused even to read any department memos about the workings of the system, his theory being cops shouldn't pass notes. It felt high schoolish. And, even though the tech geeks promised this new system was easier than previous renditions, it wasn't. At least not for him. But maybe this once the machine might help.

Tapping the 'sleep' button on the keyboard brought a picture of his dog, a black and white mixed-breed named Natasha, onto the screen, and a child-like grin to his lips, until his gaze trailed to the clock in the corner and he remembered he was being forced to waste time. Using his free hand, he proceeded to hunt and peck "Brooklyn New York Police Precincts," and waited for the network to respond. It was slow today, as usual.

When the listing finally appeared, there were more choices than he'd expected. Exasperated, he examined each option, hoping his brain would kick in and he'd remember which precinct Abledan said he'd worked with. Finally it did.

"Eighty-eighth precinct," he growled into the phone.

"One moment please."

A few more rings summoned another computerized, mono-toned female voice, this one asking which department in the precinct he wanted. Harris's jaw tightened. His fist tightened on the phone receiver.

"Homicide," he announced, and was rewarded with four minutes of country music.

When a feminine, almost inaudible, human voice finally answered, Harris introduced himself

"What can I do for you, Detective?"

"I've got a murder investigation going on here, and a guy who says he worked with your department a couple weeks ago."

"What's the guy's name? Who was the vic?"

"Don't know the vic, but the guy's name is Abledan, Douglas Abledan. Could you check if he has a sheet? Or maybe he's a C.I.?"

"Finding a sheet is easy, C.I's are more difficult. Hang on, please."

The phone went silent for a moment. Then, for the next five minutes, Harris's ear was assaulted by hip-hop music.

"Sorry to take so long, Detective," the woman said when she returned. "It's been busy here today. I have either good or bad news for you, depending on your perspective. I have no sheet for a Douglas Abledan."

Harris's eyebrows rose. "Nothing at all?"

"Well, I did find one thing, a two year old accident report. It seems your guy was the vic of a drive-by."

"At least that part of his story rang true," Harris mumbled.

"What was that, Detective?"

"Nothing. Thanks for your help."

Harris was about to end the call when he heard the woman began a question.

"Do you know the name of the officer in charge of the case?"

"I think his name was Henkle. Hang on, let me check my notes." He exhaled heavily. "Yep, that was it, Henkle."

After four rings, and a surprising degree of efficiency, Harris found himself connected to Henkle himself. The man's angry, gravelly voice told him he had too much on his plate. He introduced himself, and asked about Abledan.

The phone went silent, but through the dead air, Harris heard Henkle sigh. He looked at his watch. It was late in the shift. The guy was probably as tired as he was, and as sick of answering the phone.

"Never heard of him. Is he a perp?"

"No. Not yet anyway. Just someone of interest. Thanks for your help."

Harris slammed the phone down. The call hadn't been a waste of time after all. He'd caught Abledan in a lie, and, in his experience, one lie always led to another.

* * *

Dr. Dawson tried the knob on Ortega's office door. He turned his head left and right, making sure no one saw him, then slipped inside. Ortega wouldn't be returning. He'd watched the man bid the security guard at the front desk good night and exit the building. Now was his opportunity. If Ortega knew anything about the corn disease he chose not to share with the staff, as his employers intimated, there would probably be some kind of report secreted in the office.

He'd been paid well to secure any information he could, but anything he could find would also help him write a paper about the disease before the other researchers took the opportunity to do so. After all, this was his chance to show the world he was just as good, if not better, than the others. His chance to make a name for himself. He couldn't, he wouldn't, pass it up.

Ortega appeared to be fastidious about his workspace. There wasn't a pen out of place, and there were no loose papers littering the desktop. He rummaged through the drawers, but found nothing useful. Only one piece of artwork adorned the room, a framed photograph of three rowboats sitting on a deserted beach. The print stood out in the drab office. He stared at it, scratching the stubble on his chin, then carefully lifted it off the wall and placed it on the floor by his feet. A safe, with a fingerprint-reader lock, lay buried in the wall.

The corners of his chapped, thin lips curled upward. He reached into his pocket and pulled out a small sheet of clear plastic imbued with an impression of Ortega's fingerprint. He'd learned a few tricks as an industrial spy, and since he suspected the man would have some sort of security precautions in his office, he took the precaution of lifting the fingerprint from a disposed coffee cup. Carefully placing the plastic sheet over the fingerprint reader, he waited while a dim red light slid from left to right and a soft click told him the safe was unlocked.

Inside, he found a thick folder filled with sheets of lined paper covered with Cordelia's chicken-scratch handwriting.

*Now, this is interesting.*

This, he surmised, must be the information he'd been looking for, information Ortega didn't want the scientists to know. Why else hadn't the man mentioned it, and why else lock it in a safe?

Spreading the individual pages out on Ortega's desk, he used a hand scanner to copy the text and send it to his computer. Then, before leaving the office, he replaced the folder, closed the safe, and repositioned the print on the wall; secure in the knowledge his employers would be pleased.

* * *

Luiz Garcia stood behind twenty other people waiting to present their documentation to the customs official at O'Hare international Airport. The hour was late. He felt completely drained. Nervously fumbling with his passport, he thought of the hot shower and soft bed waiting for him at the hotel.

*This is all Joan's fault. I hate this damned country.*

To Garcia's way of thinking, the Gringos, as his father used to call them, were not very pleasant people. They didn't share their wealth, or their technology for that matter. But, not being a fan himself, anyone who had it could keep it.

Finally he stood face-to-face with a heavy-set, square shouldered agent who grunted and held out a gnarled hand for Garcia's passport, which he leafed through carefully before taking a large, metal stamp off the table and pressing it against a blank page.

"Smile pretty for the camera, Sir," he said, as Garcia started to turn away.

"We photograph everyone coming through customs these days. Now, if I could get a scan of your thumb print, I'll send you on your way."

"Let's just get this over with, please."

"Yes, Sir. Just put your thumb on this plate. It will all be over in a second."

The agent pointed to a small spot on the table where the metal had been cut away to make room for a plate of glass. Garcia didn't like the look of the surface. There were greasy streaks all over it, but he complied anyway. After a moment, he heard a whirring sound as a light passed under the glass. His finger tingled.

"Thank you, Sir. You're all set. Welcome to the United States."

Garcia put the passport back in his pocket, picked up his suitcase, and walked out of the terminal. The air stank. He knew it would. The odors of technology engulfed him. The stench of unburned fuel seared his nostrils. Body odors, barely covered by the latest chemical aromas meant to mask them, made his stomach knot up. He felt surrounded by everything he hated about 21st-century living. Too much movement. Too many "advancements." Everything stank. Cars whizzed by. People milled about. He wasn't happy. And it was all Joan's fault. Well, hopefully he would be able to get his mission over quickly.

Ortega didn't want him there anyway.

* * *

Elizabeth Tuttle hurried into her apartment, taking a deep breath of the thick, minty air before closing the door behind her. The aroma of the herb garden in the corner of the living room always soothed her. Today its tranquilizing effects were more appreciated than ever. Ortega, the man she loved, the man she would do anything for, now scared her. He became more forceful, more authoritative by the day. At work he watched her every move. And, whereas he only utilized her particular skill twice before, now he wanted her to distill more poison. He gave no indication who he intended to use it on, but she would not allow herself to become his victim. Mindful of this danger, she refused to imbibe anything capable of masking its taste while in his presence.

In bed things changed, too. It wasn't that Ortega wanted sex more often-in fact, lately he accepted fewer of her advances. Their bedroom activities were now along the lines of master and slave, and she was the slave. In some ways, she knew she always had been.

Shortly after they'd first started the affair, and despite her firm intentions, she fell in love with him. She loved what he stood for. She loved the fact that he wouldn't let anything stop him from achieving a goal and, despite his recent coolness; she knew there was very little she wouldn't do for him. She had, in a word, fallen into a trap of her own making. She knew it, but either couldn't or wouldn't break free. The only thing she could do now was make sure any harm done to anyone could not be traced back to her. That, at least, was easy. She had done it before, back home.

Before she'd become an agricultural pathologist, Tuttle had been known simply as the local healer in her Appalachian Kentucky town, because she knew which herbs to give for different illnesses, an art which had been passed down in her family for generations. She enjoyed her life, and the prestige afforded to her, until the fateful day when she found herself accused of killing the wife of a powerful farmer. Humiliated, she'd run away, out of guilt and fear. When she'd changed her name, and used her skills to establish a new career for herself in the scientific world, she thought she's left her old life behind her. But, somehow Ortega found out about her past and, after first seducing her, exploited it. By the time she discovered he knew about her past it was too late. He wouldn't let go of her, and, in truth she didn't want him to.

Ortega made up some excuse for not wanting to come over tonight. For the first time in a long while, her bed felt empty, and sleep didn't come easily. Finally tossing the heavy covers off, she sat up and reached for the red flannel robe at the foot of the bed, then walked to the herb garden in her living room. Her therapist told her pruning plants would relax her, and she found it to be true.

Her collection included several varieties of fungi and

mint, among which was, of course, pennyroyal. The aroma of the plants filled the air with an intoxicating bouquet. Each served a different purpose and carried a different scent. She loved each for a different reason.

Picking up a small pair of pruning shears, she cut a sprig off one of the peppermint plants and, after saying a silent prayer of thanks to Gaia, carried the leaves into the kitchen and placed them into a large, glass mug. Filling the mug with cold water from the tap, she placed it in the microwave, and set the timer for one minute. When the machine beeped, she carried the steaming tea into the living room and plopped herself down on the couch. The vent on the side exhaled softly under her weight, making a sound akin to a sorrowful sigh, something she could relate to given her current predicament. Her thoughts drifted to Cordelia. A single tear trailed down her cheek. Finally, taking a long sip of the tea, she closed her eyes, and let the liquid's warmth radiate through her body.

Ten minutes later, with tears in her eyes, she'd reached the only conclusion she could; the only one she thought might bring her safety. Reaching up to the ceiling, she disconnected the smoke detector, then opened a drawer and took out a book of matches. The dried leaves hanging by strings, waiting to be distilled into poison, would burn mercifully quickly. The rest would suffer in the teeth of the garbage disposal.

She struck the match, sniffing in the acrid odor of sulfur, then touched the flame to each dried bunch. Finally, she minced up her still-growing babies with the pruning shears, carried the multi-colored pile to the sink, offered a prayer to Gaia, and cried while the disposal grounded it up.

Her children were all gone now, but would it be enough.

# CHAPTER TWELVE
*Day 9*

Tuttle woke uncomfortably. Sleep leaving her, she discovered she'd been bound at her wrists and ankles. The rough cloth scratched her flesh when she tried to move. Ortega loomed over her. She shielded her eyes from the sun, trying to look at him. The light glistened on tears as they began running down her face. She knew this game, a derivative of the one he played when he felt particularly upset or angry with one of his staff. He would sit in the chair behind his desk, not saying a word, with the window shade fully open. The light from the window would bathe him and blind whoever sat on the opposite side of the desk. In his mind, this gave him a godlike appearance, but the imagery didn't faze her. She had her own ghosts and demons to contend with.

"I thought you understood," Ortega shouted. "The work being done was an abomination. It had to be stopped, at any cost. You were hired to protect Gaia. I explained the mission to you. Now you've not only betrayed me, but you've also betrayed her. That cannot be tolerated. I saw the desecration you committed on your charges. I saw you murder them."

Tuttle stared at her lover through a window of tears. "You saw? How?"

"Didn't you think I took precautions? When we first started seeing each other I placed cameras in your apartment. Here, let me show you."

With a wicked grin on his lips Ortega walked to the bookcase and pushed several of the volumes aside. There, hidden from sight, sat a video camera.

"That was really a nice touch, my dear, praying for Gaia's forgiveness for what you were doing. Of course *she* won't forgive you, and neither can I."

"I'm sorry, 'nesto, honey," Tuttle sobbed. "I had no choice. I just couldn't live with myself anymore. And you were becoming so, well, obsessed. I can't be a part of it anymore."

Ortega's face turned beet red. "First, I've told you not to call me that." He growled, slapping her face with the back of his hand. "Second, you did have a choice and you made the wrong one."

"I'm sorry. You know I would never betray you."

Ortega's fingers tightened on the handle of his cane. "But you have betrayed me. We were on a mission. How will that mission be completed now?"

Tuttle's face contorted in pain. Tears fell uncontrolled down her reddened cheeks. Her hair plastered to the wet trail.

Suddenly the tip of a needle plunged into her neck, leaving a burning sensation in its wake. Fire trailed through her veins. Her body convulsed, violently straining against the ropes binding her. Then, as darkness enveloped her, she felt nothing.

* * *

Ortega waited until the woman's screams subsided, and

190

her body ceased its thrashing, before untying her and wrapping her left hand around the suicide note he preemptively typed on her office computer.

For the next twenty minutes he worked on erasing every shred of evidence indicating he had ever been in the apartment. He ran a cloth over every flat surface to destroy lingering fingerprints. He washed the glass in the bathroom, in case it held traces of his saliva. Once certain he'd covered his tracks, he lifted Tuttle's limp arm and encircled the hypodermic with the fingers of her right hand, then left the apartment without looking back.

* * *

Standing at the front door to the University of Illinois' research facility, Luiz Garcia took a deep breath. He didn't know how he would explain his arrival. He didn't even know himself why he stood there, but Joan had insisted he go. Now, he would have to confront Ernesto Ortega, whoever he was. He wasn't looking forward to the meeting. There was no doubt in his mind he could help identify and cure the corn problem, if asked to do so. But Ortega made it clear he didn't want him here. He tried to explain the situation to Joan, but she would hear none of it. She could be a very stubborn woman when she wanted to be.

Finally, he pulled open the door and walked inside. A wave of warm air hit him squarely in the face. Bright sunlight filtered in from the panes of glass on the right side of the hallway and bounced off mirrors on the opposing wall. Between the two, a lone woman sat behind a wooden desk. Garcia walked up to her, but she paid no attention to him until he cleared his throat and introduced himself.

"Do you have an appointment? Dr. Ortega doesn't usually see people without an appointment."

"No. But I believe he may be expecting me. I phoned a few days ago."

The woman picked up the phone and spoke quietly into it, all the while peering up at him, and Garcia realized his suspicions of not being welcome seemed to be justified.

"Well," she said finally, "you're right about Dr. Ortega expecting you. But he doesn't sound very happy to hear you've arrived. Nonetheless, he's instructed me to escort you to his office. Follow me, please. Dr. Ortega's office is on the top floor. He likes to look down on the world."

The woman stood, smoothing the folds of her skirt. Then, without waiting to see if he was following her, began walking down the long hallway. When they arrived at the end, she pressed a button to call the elevator.

The ride was quicker than Garcia had imagined it would be, bumpier too. Being as the earthquakes had obviously reached this city, evidenced by several uprooted trees outside; he wondered if the machinery had been thrown off kilter. He'd never liked riding in elevators, even when they were in perfect condition. They reminded him of the underground earthquake shelters, the padded cells, in which he'd always felt claustrophobic. Fortunately, after only a few moments, the doors opened. After a short walk, the woman stopped, and knocked on a heavy wooden door.

"Come in, Norah," a voice on the other side bellowed.

The door swung open with a screech.

"Mr. Garcia," Ortega bellowed, "what are you doing here? I told you we didn't need your help. But, I suppose, as long as you're here, you may as well come in and sit down. I'm sure you're tired after your long journey. Norah, you may go."

The woman turned away without a word, leaving Garcia to fend for himself.

Garcia took a seat by the desk Ortega sat behind, then opened his briefcase, and pulled out a sheet of paper.

"After I spoke to you on the phone I received a note from Dr. Cordelia, apparently written just prior to her death."

"And did this note suggest you barge in here uninvited?"

Garcia frowned. "Actually, Dr. Cordelia invited me to come here. After our conversation I knew you were not interested in speaking to me, and frankly your disinterest was enough for me."

"And yet, here you are."

"Well, my fiancee insisted. She's positive I can be of help. At the very least perhaps I can help you and your colleagues understand the history of corn."

"An interesting, though probably useless, endeavor. But, I would hate to send you back home just to get yelled at by your woman."

"Very kind of you." Garcia pulled more papers from his briefcase then set it on the floor beside him. "You know, your problem here is exactly why Mexican officials banned genetic manipulation of corn crop in 1998. Unfortunately, that ban was largely ignored."

Ortega leaned forward in his chair and fixed cold eyes on the other man.

"Is that so? Well, then, perhaps we are going in exactly

the direction Gaia wishes us to go?"

Garcia's brow furrowed. "Gaia? Who is Gaia?"

"That depends on who you ask. Some would describe Gaia as an ecological theory explaining the complex, interactive relationship between organic and inorganic components of the Earth."

"You don't hold to this theory?"

"No. I believe Gaia to be the living embodiment of the Earth. She is a goddess, constantly watching over all living things."

"Hmmm. Well, I'm afraid I'm not a believer. I suppose you could call me an atheist."

Ortega clasped his fingers tightly together. "Science and spirit, Mr. Garcia. They go hand in hand. Perhaps we are being punished for our arrogance, our lack of faith? Perhaps this corn plague is Gaia's way of showing her children the errors of their ways."

Garcia was taken aback. Rarely had he met a man, purportedly a revered scientist, who showed such irrational religious fervor.

"I wouldn't go that far, Doctor. But I do think the original manipulation, and successive genetic 'alterations', have produced this current plague. Did you know, in 2001 researchers from the University of California discovered Mexican native corn varieties had been contaminated by engineered DNA? Or that, in the same year, genetically modified corn was discovered growing in the wild?"

"I didn't know that. But I am not sure of the relevance."

Garcia couldn't believe his ears. Was this really the man leading the search for a cure of the corn plague? Didn't he understand even the basics of genetics?

"Since 2015 almost the entire food crop of the world has been genetically engineered. I believe that engineering weakened corn's resistance to the current plague. If you need further proof just look at wheat."

"Wheat? I'm not sure I understand."

Garcia was fairly certain the man sitting before him did not want to understand, and did not want to hear, anything calling into question his so-called faith.

But, angered by Ortega's arrogance, he pressed on. He reminded Ortega about the plague in Uganda, during the first decade of the century, recalling it wiped out more than thirty percent of the world's wheat crop virtually overnight, and caused the deaths of thousands.

"That plague, we learned too late, was linked to genetic manipulation. The rust fungus had become resistant to pesticides bred into the plants." In fact it favored these plants. The same thing can, and probably will, happen to the corn crop. Humans have very short memories."

Two hours later, it was apparent Ortega, who alternatively yawned and thrummed his fingers on the desk throughout the conversation, had only pretended to listen.

When he stood up to leave, Garcia realized two things. First, this so-called scientist would continue his dangerous activities. And second, Joan had been right. It would be up to him to help find the answers Ortega refused to look for.

* * *

Dr. Lad Dawson had just stepped off the elevator on his way to his office, when he heard a loud voice coming from down the hall. Always searching for a piece of information proving useful to his employers, he crept toward the sound of the voice. Just then, the door to Ortega's office flew open, and a Hispanic man he didn't recognize stormed out.

"Bad meeting with our illustrious Dr. Ortega?"

"That man is a pompous egomaniac," Garcia shot back.

"Yep, that's our glorious leader all right. Good thing he's got the brains to go with that enormous ego, though. Otherwise, we wouldn't be the top-rated research facility in the country, I guess."

After juggling with their assorted papers, briefcases, and coffee cups, the two men introduced themselves to each other. Dawson's ears perked up when Garcia began talking about his expertise in ancient plants.

"So, are you here to join us, Dr. Garcia?"

"It's mister, at least for a little while longer, and I thought I might. I came here to offer my services after receiving a note from your Dr. Cordelia. She apparently thought my field of interest might be of value to your current project. But, it seems Dr. Ortega is adamantly opposed to any outside help on this corn plague."

Dawson recognized an opportunity when it hit him in the face. Here was a man who seemed to have information Ortega either didn't deem important, or didn't want the others to know for some reason. Either way it was an opportunity to learn more about where the plague began. He could beat the other researchers and write a paper about this, and perhaps he could find a buyer for the information too.

"Well, we definitely could use all the help we can get. Since Dr. Cordelia's death, you were told she died, weren't you? Anyway, we've been struggling a bit. And, I suppose Dr. Ortega doesn't need to know you're helping us, especially if he doesn't want you to."

The two men began walking down the hall, furiously exchanging questions.

* * *

Granger spent the rest of the morning searching through the department's database, trying to learn all he could about any progress made on the investigation into Cordelia's death. He read through Harris's notes, which focused on his suspicions about Douglas, and the line of investigation he was following based on them.

*Idiot!*

Next, he pulled up the coroner's report. Several pages of text filled the screen. Dr. Hills had a way of droning on and on, musing about his findings, not getting to the point until almost the end of the report. Granger learned long ago he needed to thoroughly study the long prose to glean any salient information buried within.

Finally, a thought came to mind. Douglas spoke about the possibility of a common aroma. At the time, he dismissed the notion as the ramblings of a desperate man grasping at straws. But maybe there was something to it.

Granger cracked his knuckles and began to punch key words into the database's search engine, hoping to cross check any recent deaths having to do with plants of any kind. The computer whizzed away busily before presenting a single hit on the screen. A woman whose body had been found outside Capone's restaurant supposedly died with mushrooms in her stomach. Though it was not uncommon to find a body with food in its stomach, especially outside a restaurant, a lightbulb flashed in his mind. Many varieties of mushrooms are poisonous.

*Douglas was going to interview a waitress at Capone's. Harris is going to have a field day with this.*

Within moments, he was gripping the steering wheel of his Prius, on his way toward the Cook County coroner's office. Traffic on the Eisenhower Expressway was light, but, because of the earthquakes, there was always construction going on. Still, with any luck, he would get there before Harris learned what Douglas was up to.

At the Ashland Avenue intersection, Granger looked up at the condominiums and envisioned his wife preparing lunch for the children. Tosha wouldn't appreciate that he was trying to do an end run around Harris, but she would certainly approve of him trying to keep the blind man out of trouble.

When he finally arrived at the coroner's office, and found the door open, Granger let himself in.

"I hope I'm not coming at a bad time, Dr. Hills. I need to ask you a question about a body you recently examined."

Hills looked up from the page he was reading. Peering over his reading glasses, the flesh between his eyes wrinkled, he tried to focus on the man who had entered his office.

"I'm Sergeant Michael Granger. You might have known my father."

Hills's eyebrows rose.

"Granger? Hmm. Oh yes, I knew a patrolman by that name. I was sorry to hear about his death."

"Thank you. It happened a long time ago. He died on the job. A family tradition I hope not to follow."

Hills nodded. "What can I do for you, son?"

"You worked on a woman recently..."

"Please, you'll have to be more specific. I work on more than my share of women. Unfortunately, they're all dead."

Granger cleared his throat. "Yes, but, well, this one was young."

"Most of them are, unfortunately."

"This one happened just a few days ago," Granger continued, undaunted by Hills's interruptions. "Your report listed mushrooms in her stomach. I was wondering if you had determined a cause of death yet. Have you identified the variety of mushroom?"

Hills frowned, clearly puzzled.

"Might I ask your interest in this case?"

"I'm working on a case where the victim was poisoned, using a toxic plant, and I'm wondering about a possible connection."

"I see. I'm afraid such things are within your purview, not mine. But hang on a sec. Let me look something up."

Hills walked to a workstation and typed furiously.

"The body was found downtown yesterday, outside Capone's?"

"That's it!"

The edges of Hills's lips turned upward slightly.

"I love that place. Reminds me of the old gangster days. Great music too."

"You were saying about the woman?"

"Well, according to my notes, she was strangled. There was a long, wide, concave depression on her neck. I found several small paint chips in the wound, probably left by the murder weapon. I also found several fibers, of two varieties, under her fingernails. The first were dark blue, perhaps from a suit coat. The others were silk, probably a shirt.

"Her death was quick, but not too quick. She fought back. I wish she'd had skin instead of fibers under her nails so we could have tried a DNA search, but perhaps whatever her assailant was wearing was too thick. In any event, I'm guessing her attacker ended up with scratches somewhere on his body."

The coroner went on to describe, in rather more technical detail than Granger wanted, the condition of the body. The woman's eyes exhibited petechial hemorrhages around the eyeball, due to an elevation of pressure within the small blood vessels. He finished his report by describing the condition of her vertebra, snapped at the third cervical level, and her hyoid bone, nearly crushed.

"Whoever her assailant was, he almost took her head clean off. He'd have had to be very strong to do that, and very angry I'd think. I told all this to Detective Harris, but there's more, if you'd care to hear it."

"Of course," Granger replied, though he knew, almost as soon as he'd said it, that anymore technical jargon threatened to put him to sleep. Still, he reasoned, anything he could learn about this woman's death would help to solve the case.

"The detectives on the scene suspected a rape-murder," Hills said, as he continued to read off the computer. "But, I found no evidence of recent sexual activity. Furthermore, from the position and severity of the wound, the murderer would have had to have been standing behind her. In my experience, most rapists don't attack from behind. They enjoy seeing terror in their victim's eyes."

Granger understood, all too well, the pattern Hills described to him. He'd investigated many such crimes during his career, and they all had one thing in common. Even after death, the look of terror often remained in the victim's eyes.

"I did find something else of interest when I looked inside the body," Hills continued, pulling Granger from his thoughts. "She had eaten shortly before she was killed, and there were undigested mushrooms in her stomach. Something told me to do a tox screen, probably because at the time I was thinking of another, recent murder. Anyway, the test came back positive."

"So, she was strangled *and* poisoned? Talk about overkill. No pun intended."

Hills didn't crack a smile, leaving Granger to wonder if the coroner even heard his remark.

"The phalloidin would have killed her eventually, probably six to fifteen hours after ingestion, though I've read about cases where death has taken as long as forty- eight hours. Apparently, the murderer didn't feel like waiting. Unfortunately, Detective Harris didn't either. He stormed out of here before I could finish my report. All he heard about was the strangulation."

*Sounds like Harris. Going off half-cocked before he knows the whole story.*

Now Granger had more of a reason to follow up on this case, to protect Abledan. The blind man was walking right into Harris's trap, but he was not going to be implicated in this murder, not if Granger had anything to say in the matter. He'd put his career on the line in the past for far less.

* * *

Granger squirmed in the Naugahide chair. His brow was damp, but he couldn't tell if it was due to the room's temperature, or because Harris sent a messenger to retrieve him, as though he were a student being summoned to the principal's office. Now, the overzealous detective sat across from him behind a heavy oak desk strewn with overturned coffee cups and papers. His back turned to Granger, he barked into the telephone.

Granger told himself to relax. Harris could do him no harm. Since he was not under the detective's command, he could have refused to heed the summons. But, the man had been investigating Cordelia's death and, because he promised to help Abledan, he felt compelled to speak to him whenever "permitted" to do so.

"It seems you've been duped," Harris boomed, as he swiveled his chair around. "Duped, patrolman. Taken for a ride. Deceived by your buddy, Abledan."

"It's Sergeant, actually, but you knew that already. And I still don't understand. How exactly did Mr. Abledan deceive me?"

Harris cleared his throat. His steely gaze pierced into Granger like a laser beam.

"Your buddy Abledan has been lying to everyone except me, it seems. He is not now, and has never been, Cordelia's 'boyfriend.' He's only said so in an effort to stay close to the case, to make sure no one suspects him. Apparently your mystic powers of detection have failed you."

And you know this how exactly?

"I paid Abledan a visit at his hotel. I asked him for the truth. He gave it to me. It's really quite simple. You just have to know how to ask the right questions. You'll learn how to do it someday, maybe. I suggest you have another conversation with him. But, before you do, you might want to read up on interview techniques, especially the part about not getting emotionally involved."

"Thanks for the sage advice, Harris," Granger said, rising from the chair. He might have been summoned by this pompous man, but he had no intention of giving Harris the suggestion he had the power to dismiss him. "You don't mind if I check this out for myself, do you?"

"No, please go right ahead. And, while you're at it, you might want to consider that Abledan also told me he'd worked a murder case in cooperation with the New York City police. I doubted it, but I called all the same. As I'd suspected, they have no record of it or him. Perps tend to lie. Some of them even try to make themselves look like innocent victims."

"I'll keep that in mind, Detective. Now, if you'll excuse me, I have a phone call to make. Real police work. You understand, I'm sure. And, thanks again for your advice. I love these little chats. We must have them more often. I don't know how I survived without them. Oh, one more thing. I spoke to the coroner, Dr. Hills a short time after you did. Apparently, he didn't get a chance to tell you the woman whose murder you discussed with him, Lucy Tanner, had poison mushrooms in her stomach. He told me she would have died from them if the murderer hadn't gotten impatient."

Harris leaned forward, staring at Granger with fire in

his eyes.

"That doesn't mean Abledan couldn't have killed her. I've told you before, people can learn about all sorts of things on the Internet, even about poisons. People lie, Patrolman. It's best to keep that in mind."

With bile rising in his throat, Granger stormed out of the room. Harris was not going to give up and, as much as he hated to admit it, he needed to give the detective credit for one thing. He'd taken for granted that a man in Abledan's position, a man whose world was partially obscured, would tell the truth simply to keep the rest from becoming an illusion. Now, he had to wonder if Abledan was hiding something.

* * *

The coffee shop was busier than on Douglas's two previous visits. Sniffing the air, he could swear he smelled cigarette smoke despite the decades-old ban on them in public buildings. The noxious odor was partly masked by the coffee and warm apple pie he'd ordered, but it was there.

When Sergeant Granger announced himself, Douglas rose, extended his hand, and then listened as a chair scraped along the floor.

"It's good to see you again," he said, as he took his seat. "I trust you have information for me, something more about Cara's death?"

"Not exactly, no. I understand Detective Harris paid you a visit."

Douglas's smile disappeared. There was a directness, a coldness, in Granger's voice not present in their previous conversations.

"He asked me questions about my relationship with Cara. You were right, by the way. He is a completely unpleasant man."

"You told him there was no relationship between the two of you," Granger said, harshly. "You told him you were lying to people, as a tool to help you get information. Isn't that right? You lied to me, as you've lied to others, to cover your own tracks."

Douglas blinked his dead eyes. He couldn't believe the one time he'd chosen to believe a policeman might actually be helpful to him he was, once again, disappointed.

"My tracks? Am I to understand you consider me a suspect now also? I assure you, I intended only to learn the truth. I didn't lie, not exactly. Though, I admit to exaggerating somewhat. But if you'd had my experience in the past you would have done the same thing. People are not forthcoming in even the most dire circumstances."

"I know that. All cops do. But you've placed me in a very uncomfortable position. And frankly, your actions make the cop in me very suspicious."

"I understand your reservation. Were our situations reversed, I might feel the same way. But Cara is still dead. Her killer is still loose. And, I still need your help. I'm sorry I misrepresented myself, but I didn't see another option. My past experience, both with police and witnesses, is the truths of the world are often hidden. You can't possibly understand how that feels to a blind man. Too many things are hidden from me even now."

"The truth is often hidden, from everyone, Douglas. I'm not following your reasoning."

Douglas drew in a deep breath before continuing. "Before I was blinded I worked with numbers. I saw the world in a certain way. I recognized patterns in how things looked, in how they added up. Since losing my sight, I've lost the ability to see those patterns. The truths they showed me have been obscured. I've had to rely on other methods in order to regain a sense of order in my life."

"I think I understand. I can't begin to imagine living with your loss. But, lying is not the way to deal with it. Lying makes you look guilty, of something. It further obscures the world you're trying to clarify. If I'm to help you find your sense of order, at least as it pertains to the death of Dr. Cordelia, you must be honest. With everyone."

"I apologize for any trouble I may have caused you."

"You've caused yourself trouble too, Douglas. And I'm concerned about that, deeply. You told Harris you'd worked with the New York City police, on a murder investigation? But, according to Harris, there is no record of that."

Douglas's jaw dropped. "But, that's impossible. It was an important case, the death of John Haggarty, the president of Unimat. I found his murderer for them and, in point of fact, almost got killed in the process."

"I read about the case. But Douglas, I'm telling you there is no record of your being involved. And, you saying you were just adds another piece of evidence to Harris's view that you're a liar, and possibly a murderer. And now there have been other murders possibly related to Dr. Cordelia, and to you."

Douglas didn't know how to respond. He'd always heard the police didn't like to share the glory when they solved cases, and here was proof.

"I'm very sorry to hear that. Obviously, I had nothing to do with any of those deaths."

"I'm afraid it isn't obvious to Detective Harris. In fact, what makes this more difficult is he knows you went to see one of the victims. He knows you left the woman in tears. And, if I know Harris, I'm positive he suspects you had something to do with her death as well as Dr. Cordelia's."

Douglas thought about the people he interviewed. Each of them lied to him, or withheld some piece of information. The flight attendant abruptly ended their conversation when he'd gone to see her. Ortega sweated profusely, and lied about an injury he'd sustained. Even Dr. Tuttle, who was supposedly Cordelia's friend, seemed nervous when speaking about her.

But, of them all, the woman at Capone's, Lucy Tanner, seemed the most compassionate, and especially distraught, after hearing about Cordelia's death. If he understood what Granger was telling him, she was now dead too, and he was being blamed. Someone was trying to tie up loose ends, and throwing suspicion onto him in the process.

"I'm not sure how to dissuade him. When all is said and done I am positive I'll be able to prove my innocence, and I'll be able to show both of you who the real murderer is."

"I hope you're right, Douglas. As I've said before, I know Harris very well. He's a bloodhound. When his nose points to something he sticks to it, and he'll stick to you until he has proven his case. I can't emphasize enough my feeling you should distance yourself from this mess, and from Harris. I would tell you to go back home, but in good conscience I can't do that anymore. Not while Harris is investigating you. But, do us both a favor, please. Just try to stay out trouble."

"I'm sorry, but I can't make any promises. But, you might want to tell that detective of yours when I spoke with one of Cara's associates, a Dr. Tuttle, I noticed the same smell on her that accompanied a cup of tea a flight attendant had served Cara on our way to Chicago.

I went to see her-the flight attendant, I mean-to tell her about Cara's death, and to ask if she'd noticed anything odd about the aroma of the tea. She said she didn't, but she didn't seem terribly upset by the news either. In fact, she quickly excused herself and left the building."

Douglas went on to explain he'd noticed the same aroma in the drink served by Lucy Tanner at Capone's. And, it was the reason he'd gone to speak with her.

"I don't know what it all means yet, but it seems significant. Don't you agree?"

"I agree you've got a very sensitive nose, Douglas. And, there seems to be a lot to this series of events Harris is ignoring. I'll pass all of this information on, but I'm not sure it will do any good. I'm not even sure if what you've said you smelled would stand up as evidence in a court of law. Actually, I don't really know why I've gotten myself so involved with you, but I have. So, of course, I'll do whatever else I can for you. But Douglas, for your own sake, stay out of the way. Harris is on a witch hunt."

"So you've said, and I appreciate you looking out for me. Speaking of my sense of smell, there's one more thing. I don't know where, or if, it fits. The last time I met with Ernesto Ortega I smelled blood in the air. It was faint, but definitely present. I asked him if he had cut himself shaving. He told me a story about being injured while working out at his dojo. I called to check his story, because it didn't seem likely. Sure enough, the instructor, a man named Thomans, by the way, didn't know anything about Ortega being injured. Obviously he lied to me, though I don't know why." When Granger didn't immediately respond, Douglas became concerned. But, when the policeman finally told him about the conversations he'd had over the last several days, including the most recent one with the coroner, Dr. Hills, he realized another piece of his puzzle just fell into place. Ortega had indeed been scratched by a woman with sharp fingernails-Lucy Tanner. Obviously they had some sort of relationship, and not a pleasant one, if the scratches she'd inflicted on him were any indication. But there were still pieces missing. The picture was not yet complete, and until it was neither he nor the detective, Harris, would rest.

# CHAPTER THIRTEEN
*Day 10*

The ringing of the phone shook Douglas from yet another nightmare. He reached over to the nightstand, pushing a button on the clock.

"The time is now eight o'clock. Good morning," the automated voice announced, with a cheerfulness that made him wince.

He pulled the receiver to his ear just in time to hear a wheezing cough. It was Sid, back in New York, the last person he wanted to hear from.

"Do you have any idea how crazy this guy, Faggan, is driving me, Doug?"

As usual, the man started rambling, without bothering with pleasantries.

"That Brogue of his is enough to drive anyone insane if they listen long enough."

"Just tell him I'll get to his project as soon as I get back to New York. Tell him I'll be home in a few more days."

This was the reason Douglas hadn't wanted to hear from his boss. He didn't want to hear about the Irishman he'd met, under duress. And, he didn't want to hear anything about cutting his vacation, or his investigation, short.

"But that's just it, Doug. This guy doesn't want to wait 'a few more days.' In fact, he keeps asking me why I can't order you home now, or at least assign someone else to his project."

"I trust you've explained you can't simply order me to end my vacation? You've told him, since he's already explained his project to me, it would not make much sense to explain the whole thing all over again to someone else, haven't you?"

It was a relief to finally take a firm stand. Becoming involved in this investigation had happened haphazardly. Now two women were dead, one of which he might have grown to love, and he was the prime suspect. His reputation, and perhaps his life, were at stake. But, the pieces were finally coming together. He couldn't stop now.

"Of course I told him all that. I even told him you'd devote all your time to his one project from the very moment you got back to the office. What can I tell you? The guy is a dynamo."

"I'm sorry, Sid. I'll be here another few days. That's all. Tell him if he can't deal with that, he'll have to find another company. If you can't deal with it, then maybe you should find yourself another employee, which of course you won't do because you wouldn't want me working for a competitor. I'm making full use of my entire vacation, so I can be fresh when I come back to work. Who knows when you'll let me go on another one? Okay, I'm going back to sleep and you're hanging up the phone. Good bye, Sid."

Douglas realized he would not have spoken to his boss in such a manner if he had been fully awake. But, after he pushed the phone back down, he was glad he did. Now he could finish what he'd started. There were only a few more pieces in this puzzle. He might not be able to see the final picture, but he could smell it. The strange, minty smell would lead him to the puzzle's creator.

* * *

Sergeant Granger sat in the same chair he had occupied the day before. He took a long pull on the *grande* cup of coffee he'd bought from the Starbucks around the corner. The dark, caramel-flavored liquid had cooled off since he'd first sat down. Now it was just the right temperature to drink.

Once again, Harris was on the phone, ignoring him. He stared past the hulking figure of the detective. On the wall behind him hung a wooden plaque he hadn't noticed before. Squinting, he read the inscription "Thou Shalt Not Kill (Exodus 20:13)."

Granger had never dreamed Harris was the kind of man to display biblical quotations in his office. Everyone he'd ever spoken to about the man thought of him as a seeing-is-believing kind of guy. For Harris, evidence was only derived from hard facts leading toward absolutes. Spirituality required some degree of faith. Harris didn't seem to have any. He didn't trust anyone. That, of course, would have required faith in human nature. But, if such a man, such a cop, were going to have a biblical quote adorning his wall, it would be this.

Harris pushed the phone onto its cradle, then swirled the chair around.

"Now, Patrolman, what was it you were saying before we were interrupted?"

"I was saying I think you've set your sights on the wrong man for both the Cordelia and Tanner murders."

Harris grunted. "More of your 'mystical' powers of

reasoning, Granger?"

Granger bowed his head for a moment, concentrating on his breathing in an attempt to rein in his temper so he could look Harris straight in the eye.

"If you'd followed each of these cases logically you'd see the facts just don't add up. Cordelia was poisoned. The poison used was rare. Tanner also was poisoned, using another herbal toxin."

The corners of Harris's lips inched downward. "I hate to disagree with you, Patrolman, but Miss Tanner was strangled. I saw her body up close and personal. Even if her neck didn't have a deep horizontal depression to prove it, our esteemed medical examiner, Dr. Hills, told me that was the cause of death. The force of the pressure on her neck crushed her windpipe and hyoid bone and nearly severed her spinal column."

"I spoke to Dr. Hills as well. According to him, you didn't hear his entire report. He told me you rushed out of his office after hearing what you thought you needed. If you had waited a bit, you'd have learned Hills found mushrooms in her stomach. He did a toxicology screening and found a poison called phalloidin in her blood stream. She was strangled, but the strangulation only sped her death. He told me the poison alone would have killed her in a few hours. Apparently the perp was as impatient as you are."

Harris shrugged, clearly unimpressed. "Your friend Abledan could have done all this. I've told you before, even blind men can learn things on the Internet. What's to say he didn't harvest the plants himself and distill the poison he needed? He met with Tanner shortly before her body was found in the alleyway behind Capone's. The manager told me he saw someone matching Abledan's description leave the building, and that Tanner was in tears when he found her."

*Damn it, Douglas. Why couldn't you leave it alone?* "All good evidence, Harris. But there's more you're not considering."

Harris's eyes bugged out. "Oh?"

"According to your own report, which I read by the way, the manager said Abledan was the second person to visit Miss Tanner that day. A woman came in before he did. Apparently, she and Tanner had an explosive argument. Something about a mutual boyfriend, I think. In fact, if I remember correctly from Hills's report, Tanner's body was missing a clump of hair. This missing woman could have pulled it out during their argument. She could have been the perp. She could have set up the crime scene to look like a fouled up rape attempt."

"Would she have fed Tanner the poison mushrooms you were speaking about a moment ago as well?"

"I can't explain those, though it's possible the poisoning was accidental. After all, she was found outside a restaurant. These things have been known to happen, you know. At the very least what I've just explained has to establish some doubt in even your mind."

Harris grunted again. Granger noticed this was his usual response when he didn't want to hear something.

"Actually, it doesn't. And I think I have enough evidence, along with Abledan's propensity to lie about his past, to arrest him on suspicion of murder. Have a good day, Patrolman."

Turning his attention to a stack of papers on his desk,

Harris began to whistle. Granger was sorely tempted to slam the door behind him. Harris was about to blow this investigation, unless he could run interference, fast.

* * *

Ortega stared at the phone's caller ID. Douglas Abledan was calling, again. He'd thought he'd put enough obstacles in the blind man's path, but the man just wouldn't give up.

"Douglas? No, Elizabeth isn't here. She's taken off."

"Taken off? You mean she's taken the day off?"

"No. She was supposed to come in to work today. She knew we're on the brink of a breakthrough. It's actually an exciting time here. But she isn't answering her phone, and she hasn't been heard from since leaving the lab yesterday."

"Have you called the police? Has anyone gone to her home?"

"There's really no need. Elizabeth has a tendency to disappear now and then, for unexplained reasons. I've known her for years. She's got a very mysterious life-story. She does this kind of thing now and then. It's unprofessional, I know, but I always cover for her. Besides, if I were to phone the police every time she ran off, they'd tell me there's a forty-eight hour delay in filing missing person's reports."

"Could you tell me where she lives, then? I really do need to ask her a few questions. I wouldn't press the issue, but the things I need to know are time sensitive."

"I'm uncomfortable giving out personal information about an employee."

"I understand. But, I really do need to do this. Please. I'm running out of time. I have to go back to New York in a day or two. I need to find out what happened to Cara before I leave."

Ortega thought for a moment. The woman's body would be found, eventually, anyway. That wasn't a problem. He was sure the "suicide" looked real enough. But, he didn't like the idea of this man being the one to find her. Douglas was, if anything, too tenacious. If a piece was missing from the puzzle, he thought, he was the kind of man who wouldn't give up until he fit it into the final picture. Finally, though, ego won out over logic. Ortega refused to believe he could have left anything to chance. There was nothing left to be found he hadn't thought of first.

"To be totally honest with you, I'd appreciate some outside investigation. Something about this disappearance feels different from past instances."

Ortega leaned back. The trail of death was about to lead straight to Douglas. The blind man who sought a murderer would, himself, be charged with the murder. He couldn't help but laugh at the irony.

* * *

Douglas rang the bell on Elizabeth Tuttle's apartment door, then waited a few minutes. There was no answer. He knocked. Still no answer.

"Dr. Tuttle," he called out, raising his voice just loud enough to be heard through the door. "It's Douglas Abledan. I'd like to speak with you."

If Ortega told him the truth about the young woman's habit of disappearing on occasion, she might, he realized, not be home. On the other hand, this was the first place to

216

look for her. And, there was another worrisome factor, the now-familiar smell was coming from inside the apartment.

It didn't take much to convince the superintendent there might be a problem in Tuttle's apartment. Surrounding tenants constantly complained about the aroma Douglas mentioned and he was, he said, planning on checking it out anyway. Douglas called Granger, who told him to wait for his arrival before doing anything, but the superintendent was not a patient man. He didn't see the need to wait for the police before checking out a potential problem in his own building. Furthermore, the management company didn't like the police meddling in what they viewed as private matters.

When Tuttle's door swung open, the smell became almost overpowering, mixed as it was with another Douglas immediately recognized, death.

"Dr. Tuttle is dead," The superintendent announced. "She's here on the couch."

"It's best not to touch or disturb anything until the police arrive."

"Don't worry, I've been through these things before. We don't get many dead people here, but after you've been in this business as long as I have, you see them now and then. A real shame, it is. She was a nice lady too. Sweet, ya know. Didn't bother nobody, 'cept for the smell, of course. Never woulda suspected she was a druggie."

"What do you mean?"

"She's holding a hypodermic needle. Looks like she left a note too."

* * *

Ten minutes later, when Granger arrived on the scene, Harris was with him. Apparently, he had been in the room when Douglas's call came in, and insisted on tagging along.

"Chalking up another murder, Abledan?" Harris's voice felt like sandpaper in Douglas's ear.

"You can't possibly think I had anything to do with this, Detective. I called as soon as I noticed something literally didn't smell right. I'm sure you both noticed the sweet aroma of Pennyroyal in the air. It's quite pervasive. I was about to look for the source."

"Seems to me you probably called to try to hide a murder. What did you do? Convince the woman to let you into the apartment, kill her, and make it look like a suicide?"

"You've got to be kidding, Harris," Granger protested. "Even you can't think anything so warped."

"Call for forensics and the M.E. This shouldn't be hard to figure out quickly."

Harris walked over to Tuttle's body, frowned, and then picked up the paper laying beside her.

"Don't you think you should wait before you disturb the crime scene?" Granger asked.

"I'll put it back. Just had to see how good a suicide note Abledan was able to concoct. Pretty straight-forward. Couldn't think of more flowery words?"

"That's enough, Harris. You've no cause yet to suspect this isn't exactly what it looks like, a suicide."

"We'll see."

Before the forensic team arrived, and not wanting to miss out on any part of the investigation, Douglas followed Harris and Granger while they conducted a cursory search of the apartment. Using his extraordinary sense of smell to guide him, he led the group to remnants of Pennyroyal lodged in the teeth of the garbage disposal.

The centerpiece of the puzzle finally fell into place. Tuttle had distilled the poison that killed Cordelia, then tried to dispose of the evidence. Harris hadn't divulged the contents of the suicide note he'd found so, Douglas realized, he might never know the reason for the murder.

Tuttle had set one room up as a laboratory. With gloved hands, Granger rummaged through it and, along with remnants of a host of plants, found a rolodex with Ortega's name in it. That wasn't surprising. He was, after all, her boss. But of note was the fact that his name, and only his name, was surrounded by a series of small hearts.

"Interesting," Harris growled, without bothering to hide the disappointment in his voice. "But this doesn't prove anything."

"Sergeant," Douglas piped in, "didn't you tell me your medical examiner found fibers under Lucy Tanner's fingernails? And that, in reading Detective Harris's notes, you learned she'd had an argument with a woman over some supposed relationship?"

"Right on both counts, Douglas."

"I'm not a professional like you two gentlemen but, given what we've found here, it seems to me the other woman was likely Dr. Tuttle."

Harris mumbled his agreement.

"I suggest that the blood I smelled on Dr. Ortega, and the fibers found under Ms. Tanner's fingernails, might both have been the result of some sort of spat caused by a lover's triangle. Ortega lied when I asked him about it. And, now we know the aroma I kept smelling came from Pennyroyal, and we know Dr. Tuttle was growing it."

As he spoke, Douglas realized he would be perfectly happy if he never smelled the sweet aroma again. It would forever remind him of Cordelia, and her murder.

When the group returned to the living room, they discovered Ortega had let himself into the apartment. He told them after Douglas's call, he'd become concerned for the woman's well-being and thought it best to visit the apartment himself.

Surprised, but pleased, by the new addition, Granger peered at Harris. "Shall I put the cuffs on him, or would you like to?"

* * *

"The lab techs on the scene did an analysis with hand-held scanners," Hills began. "Unless this young lady decided at the last moment she needed help to end her life, she was murdered. And, the killer made a mistake. The scans show a man pushed the plunger on the hypo."

"Prints?" Harris's question held an eager exuberance.

Granger glowered. "Still trying to pin this on Mr. Abledan?"

"There are traces of perspiration," Hills continued. "Definitely male. Hispanic. DNA comparison with the man you arrested will show if you've got your murderer. From a personal perspective, I hope you have. These were gruesome murders. The perpetrator was a monster. Oh, Detective, at Sergeant Granger's suggestion, I did a quick scan of Mr. Abledan. He definitely is not the man in question. His DNA does not match."

220

Harris glared at the medical examiner, his eyes burning with subdued anger.

"You're sure?"

"The equipment is calibrated to follow International DNA Advisory Board standards. The margin for error is quite small."

Harris closed his eyes and sighed.

# PART THREE

## The Blues

# CHAPTER FOURTEEN

Sergeant Michael Granger spent the morning answering questions, ostensibly, about his participation in the events leading up to the arrest of Dr. Ernesto Ortega. What his superiors really wanted to know, though, was the role Douglas Abledan played. They weren't happy about a civilian, especially a blind civilian, being involved. Much to Granger's chagrin, they had little trouble expressing their displeasure, despite the fact the case might not have been solved without Abledan's persistence and independent footwork.

Granger endured one dressing down after another. In the end, it was made clear, due to what his superiors considered gross misjudgment; any thoughts of promotion should be dismissed, at least for the foreseeable future. Still, in his own mind, helping Abledan had been the right thing to do.

Now, with information he'd received from the forensics lab, he made his way to the Bureau of Investigative Services. Tosha might not have approved of what he was about to do, she'd say it wasn't a very spiritual act, but finally having the ammunition to stick it to Harris presented an opportunity he just couldn't pass up. Finally, he stopped to catch his breath, then knocked on the detective's door.

"Come in," Harris barked.

Granger opened the door slowly, peering into the room

before deciding it was safe to enter.

"I thought you should know, Detective, I've spoken to the forensics team leader. The boys found the remains of Amanita mushrooms, amongst other herbs, in Dr. Tuttle's garbage disposal. They told me Amanita are among the most deadly varieties of mushroom. I'm sure even you'd agree it is reasonable to assume she provided the mushrooms found in Lucy Tanner's stomach. And, since we know she had a relationship with Ernesto Ortega, we can further assume he was the one to use them to kill Ms. Tanner."

"Okay, Okay," Harris grumbled, as he looked up from his computer screen. "I suppose you've proven your point, Patrolman. Abledan wasn't involved, in any of the murders."

Granger grinned. "So you agree it was a good idea to help him? After all, were it not for Douglas's investigation of Cara Cordelia's death, we might not have captured Ortega."

"Yeah, yeah. You can wipe the stupid smile off your face and leave now, Patrolman. I've got work to do."

"With pleasure. Oh, but there is one last thing. It's *Sergeant* Granger, Dammit!"

He slammed the door behind him.

* * *

Detective Paul Harris was angry. He'd been shown up by a subordinate, one he hated, no less. Granger had solved *his* case, assisted by the blind man he thought of as the key suspect. Now, Ortega would pay for the embarrassment he had caused.

When he pulled Ortega into an interrogation room later

that day, he was determined to get the man to confess and, in doing so, exculpate himself from the feeling his judgment had been called into question.

By the time the interview concluded, six hours later, Ortega had outlined his entire scheme, and implicated both Dr. Cordelia's assistant, Joshua Dorn, and the airline attendant, Liz Ito. He'd actually tried to pin the entire plan on Dorn, but Harris finally managed to get the truth out of him.

It seemed they'd all cooked up some hair-brained idea that, by killing Cordelia, they'd stop scientists from finding a cure for the corn plague, and they'd garner the favor of some "mystical" force called Gaia. It all sounded kind of kooky to Harris, but then, most of the motives he'd ever heard of for murders did. As for the other murder victims, Lucy Tanner and Elizabeth Tuttle, Ortega admitted he orchestrated their deaths because he considered them to be "unfortunate but necessary."

Harris had two final tasks before he could close the case. Picking up the phone, he called the police department in Ithaca, NY, to request permission to come and arrest Joshua Dorn, then he called Delta Airlines to locate and arrest Liz Ito.

* * *

Camera men and reporters crowded into the conference room at the University of Illinois's research facility, all scrambling to get the best vantage point. At the front of the room, before an array of microphones, stood Dr. Lad Dawson and Luiz Garcia. Dawson leaned forward, then tapped on one of them.

"Ladies and Gentlemen, we are here to commemorate an auspicious event, an event the world has been desperately awaiting. Working with notes left by the late Dr. Cara Cordelia, and in collaboration with Mr. Luiz Garcia, from the University of Mexico," Dawson patted the other man's shoulder, "we've developed a way to stop the corn plague."

On the plane, flying back home from his "vacation" in Chicago, Douglas looked forward to resuming his normal routine.

*These vacations are more stressful than my work. Who needs them?*

Sitting back in his seat, listening to the music floating through his airline-supplied earphones, his thoughts wandered back over the past ten day's events. He'd become involved in multiple murders, for the second time in so many years. He'd been forced to risk his own life, again. He'd been investigated by the police, again. But, also, just as during the Haggarty affair, a cop had helped him.

*Is it possible I was wrong to lump them all together?*

As he released himself to slumber, Douglas realized the idea merited consideration.

* * *

Back at DataScan, Douglas found his office in shambles. His sonic cane virtually jumped out of his hand, as its invisible pulse struck one out of place obstacle after another. And, as if that weren't bad enough, on his answering machine he found at least a dozen messages from Faggan.

As quickly as he could, he made his way to Sid Coltrane's office. Sucking in a lungful of clean air, he pushed open the door and stormed into the smoke-filled room.

"Can't I get just one day to ease back into the grind, Sid?"

"Hey, Doug, welcome back. Find everything you need in your office?"

Douglas stared at his boss through his dead eyes, hoping in some way they would reveal his anger.

"What the hell is all that stuff doing in there?"

"Faggan. He said you requested it. The project I sent you to Chicago to find out about, remember?"

"You didn't...oh, never mind. What about all the messages he left?"

"Yeah, well. The man is persistent. What can I tell you?"

"Hmm. You could tell me that someone else in this office had the nerve to stand up to the guy. You could tell me my coworkers had my back while I was taking a much needed vacation and that someone at least sorted through the material."

"Yup. I could. In fact, the decodes are on your computer, Doug. I guess the tech guys also wanted to give you all the paperwork Faggan sent. Anyway, now that you're nice and rested from living it up in Chicago, do me a favor and finish this project before Faggan calls back. The man gives me a headache."

*"Now you know what he did to me in Chicago."* Maybe
*dealing with murders is easier than my regular life after all.*

## *IN THE END*

The rebuilt Stateville Correctional Center stood two miles north of Joliet, Illinois. Because it stood as the last remaining panopticon-style prison in the United States, the remnants of the old building, which had been destroyed by an earthquake a year earlier, were preserved. The new edifice was a combination of twentieth-century brick and mortar and twenty-first century Plasteel. Ernesto Ortega was its most recent resident.

Sitting in his cell, he studied the place where he would spend the rest of his life. He was unimpressed. The paint had already yellowed and chipped off the walls in many places. In the upper reaches of the small cell long strands of spider silk swayed in the gentle air current. His bed was a simple memory-foam mat covered with a thin blanket.

Ortega thought about the course of events that brought him to this place. He thought about the murders he'd either committed or orchestrated. He thought about the betrayals, all of them worthwhile. He felt proud of his accomplishments, and he knew Gaia was proud of him, too. Long ago he'd vowed to protect her. From that moment on, he was bound and determined to do so, no matter what the cost. And, he decided now, the cost had not been very high. It was unfortunate several people needed to die, of course. He hadn't counted on that when he took on this mission but, when he truly thought about them, he realized they deserved their fate. They hadn't treated the Earth well. They hadn't left Gaia to her own devices.

Ortega couldn't believe how few people understood what he was trying to do. Lucy hadn't had to, of course. She was a mere pawn, a means of delivery no more important than the cane he'd used to break her neck. He thought Elizabeth had understood but, he now realized, he was wrong to put his faith in her. A frightened child, she acted out of fear. In the end, there was no choice but to kill her, to protect himself and his mission. Few would understand why he'd done what he'd done, but it didn't matter. Gaia was safe.

* * *

Orlando Hernandez had been listening to the radio when he'd heard the scientists finally found a cure for the corn disease that ruined his life. He'd heard the cure would be spread throughout his country and others, at the United Nations' expense, by airplane.

Now he stood in the middle of his devastated cornfield looking up at the sky, waiting. His wife and children begged him to come inside, but he could not. The cure was coming, he kept telling them. He had to witness it in person.

Suddenly, the unmistakable sound of a small plane engine pierced the still air. Hernandez smiled and crossed himself. This could be what he'd waited for. When he saw the plane at the far edge of his land, and watched as it began to puff a bluish-white cloud out of its tail end, he fell to his knees on the damp soil and thanked God. Now he could grow his corn again. Now he could feed his family again.

Finally, he went back into his house.

www.ingramcontent.com/pod-product-compliance
Lightning Source LLC
Chambersburg PA
CBHW050506160726
48003CB00001B/193